THE THYROID MAN

THE THYROID MAN

An Autobiography

JOHN LAZARUS

MA., MD. (Cambridge) MB ChB (Glas.) BChir. (Cantab)
FRCP (Lon. Edin. Glas.) FRCOG, FACE FLSW

© John Lazarus, 2024

Published by John Lazarus

All rights reserved. No part of this book may be reproduced, adapted, stored in a retrieval system or transmitted by any means, electronic, mechanical, photocopying, or otherwise without the prior written permission of the author.

The rights of John Lazarus to be identified as the author of this work have been asserted in accordance with the Copyright, Designs and Patents Act 1988.

A CIP catalogue record for this book is available from the British Library.

ISBN 978-1-5262-1008-1

Book layout and cover design by Clare Brayshaw

Cover image www.dreamstime.com

Prepared and printed by:

York Publishing Services Ltd
64 Hallfield Road
Layerthorpe
York YO31 7ZQ

Tel: 01904 431213

Website: www.yps-publishing.co.uk

To Maureen

Contents

Chapter 1	Early Years	1
Chapter 2	Post war	5
Chapter 3	Schooldays	10
Chapter 4	Gap year	16
Chapter 5	University of Cambridge	24
Chapter 6	University of Glasgow	34
Chapter 7	University of Glasgow - Clinical Studies	37
Chapter 8	Residencies	41
Chapter 9	Start of Medical Career	47
Chapter 10	Welsh National School of Medicine	55
Chapter 11	New York - Columbia University	60
Chapter 12	The Doldrums	67
Chapter 13	Arrival of Reg	71
Chapter 14	Abu Dabi	74
Chapter 15	Senegal – A Goitre Study	77
Chapter 16	Clinical Thyroid Studies	82
Chapter 17	The Children	88
Chapter 18	The Health Service	91

Chapter 19	Teaching	97
Chapter 20	Retirement (1)	100
Chapter 21	Retirement (2)	104
Chapter 22	The End Game	107
Chapter 23	The Family	108
Acknowledgements		128

CHAPTER 1

Early Years

I was born on 12th November 1941 at 4 am in a nursing home in the West end of Glasgow. The attending obstetrician was the Regius Professor of Obstetrics and Gynaecology and I think he supervised the labour satisfactorily because I am still here and had no significant damage during the birth. In those days Glasgow was prone to serious fogs which, in addition to wartime traffic restrictions, meant that the few private cars which were permitted could not safely function. I understand that my father walked the 5 or so miles home to the South side of the city (where his house was) after the birth. I made good progress but my mother developed mastitis and was given large doses of stilboestrol to stop lactation. If this drug was to be used today the doctor would be taken to court and almost certainly be struck off the medical register.

My mother remained in the nursing home for six weeks after which the two of us returned home. My ritual circumcision was performed when I was about seven days old without adverse effect. Home was a substantial villa in the suburb of Pollokshields (see picture). It had been purchased with the help of my maternal grandfather (Emile Viner) in 1940 for £1000 prior to my parents' marriage on January 8th1941 [Obstetric calculations confirm that I was not born out of wedlock!].

52 Sherbrooke Ave, Pollokshields

Glasgow at that time was the premier centre for wartime shipbuilding along thirty miles of Clyde coast. While Britain had survived the blitz of 1940 it was losing an alarming amount of merchant ships due to enemy submarine action. Warships were not immune either. Indeed, the aircraft carrier The Ark Royal was torpedoed and eventually sank the day after I was born. On the 12th of November the Soviet 52nd Army counterattacked at Volkhov.

King George VI opened a new session of British Parliament in 1941. His speech from the throne began, "The developments of the past year have strengthened the resolution of my peoples and of my allies to prosecute this war against aggression until final victory,".

British Commandos executed Operation Astrakhan, an overnight raid on Houlgate (a small town west of Deauville) in France. The four Commandos did not encounter any Germans but did gather useful information on the suitability of the beach for use by landing craft.

Parents

My father, Samuel Lazarus, known as Sam, was a physician and medical graduate of Glasgow University.

He was born in Glasgow on 22 July 1911 the third of four children of Isaac and Rebecca Lazarus. After early education in the South side of Glasgow the family moved to Newcastle-upon-Tyne in 1921 where he attended The Royal Grammar School. He passed the matriculation exam in 1928 after which the family returned to Glasgow and he entered Glasgow University medical school graduating MB ChB with commendation in 1933. Following a medical residency (house job) in Paisley he then worked at Glasgow Royal Infirmary as a house surgeon. In the early 1930s, although the surgeons were very skilled, the speciality of anaesthetics was still in its infancy. Dad found himself in charge of administration of the anaesthetic for many operations by his boss without too much idea of how to do this. He asked the theatre sister who said, 'just pour it on doctor'! One can only imagine the trepidation involved. He undertook study for an MD degree in the Physiology department in Glasgow which involved examination of bowel function in the rat. Following his house surgeon post he was attracted to the possibility of becoming a surgeon but most of his supporters had died so that was not possible. During this time, he also gained a pass in the Membership of the Royal College of Physicians examination in London and did several locums for General practitioners in Glasgow. He then went to Copenhagen for 6 months followed by Guys Hospital in London for further study into clinical aspects of gastroenterology. It was while he was in London that he met my mother in 1938 who was more than 6 years younger. He married her in 1941. Sadly, my father's two elder siblings, a boy and a girl died young but a sister for Sam (Eve) was born on July 11, 1915.

My mother, Thelma Beatrice, was born in Sheffield to Emile and Rose Viner on April 3, 1918. After early education in Sheffield, she attended a boarding school in Eastbourne (now closed). Following a spell in Paris she went to The Chelsea Polytechnic to study botany but did not complete the degree due to the outbreak of World War 2.

The only memories I have of World War 2 are of my mother standing on the kitchen sink to adjust the compulsory blackout blind. Then I have a memory of Victory in Europe (VE) day when a huge union jack flag was placed on the roof of the porch prior to a celebration party hosted by my parents. An exciting memory for a small boy was a post war drive to the Tail O' The Bank (near Greenock on the River Clyde). There were literally hundreds of warships stretched along the river awaiting decommissioning, an awesome sight.

The other event during the war years was that my aunt Eve got married. She met a serving Surgeon Lieutenant who was the doctor to a minesweeper. The ship arrived at Glasgow for a few days and Dr Arthur Zuckerman was invited to my Grandparents house for Friday night supper where he met Eve. This general hospitality was also common in other ports in the UK during the war. I was nearly two and a half when they got married but I remember insisting that I should travel with them after the ceremony in the synagogue to the reception. I dare say there were a few raised eyebrows as I climbed out of the car! Arthur's ship was the first Royal Naval Vessel to arrive in Norway at the end of the War and received a huge welcome accompanied by large volumes of alcohol. Subsequently Arthur was notified that he had received mention in despatches with commendation in July 1944.

CHAPTER 2

Post War

The immediate post war years found a country in deep national debt with food rationing worse than during the war. In the autumn of 1945, I started in a small nursery school located a few miles from home. My only memories of this were bumping my head on a lamp post near the school and observing some of the teachers crying on the last day in summer 1947 as the school was to be closed permanently.

I proceeded from there to The Glasgow Academy (GA) in September 1947 entering the somewhat ignominiously called class 2X. This was a different environment altogether. There was a school uniform consisting of a blue blazer with the blue badge to be worn with short grey trousers, grey socks with garters and black shoes. All this was topped off with the blue GA cap. In its new state it was a very smart uniform which has stood the test of time. The school was, and still is, located in the West end of the city near the banks of the river Kelvin and close to transport facilities and the University of Glasgow. Usually, I would be dropped off in the morning by my father who was on his way to work in the Western Infirmary and collected by my mother in the mid-afternoon. In time a morning rota evolved as my second cousin Raymond lived across the road and another family were two hundred yards down the avenue. By this time aged around eight, I was allowed to come home on my own by tram. This involved walking in the direction of the university to get on the no 3 tram which took me all the way to Pollokshields without changing, a journey of forty-fifty minutes. The fare for a junior for this six mile journey was 1.5d (a penny ha'penny) I usually sat upstairs at the front in the cabin on the old-fashioned tram, sometimes with some other boys. There, we could do our homework and so be able to run out to play after we got home. The class size was around twenty five – twenty nine and I did very little or no work outside school. Schoolwork was for the most part interesting if didactic. Even at age 6 we all sat in rows in individual desks with inkwells. The ink provided a ready source of ammunition for the tip of a paper dart. Young boys love to attack and peashooters using barley (otherwise destined for soup at home) were also popular as well as catapults.

The mistresses in Junior school were required to impose a certain degree of discipline: some did this more efficiently than others and were feared by the class. Homework included spelling, arithmetic and reading. In class the next day you had to stand up to read or spell which could be a traumatic experience. The belt or tawse was a two fingered thick leather strap made in Lochgelly, a small town in Fife. It was sometimes soaked in vinegar to increase the pain and was not infrequently used to punish misdemeanours. Although this paints a Dickensian picture the boys were generally happy and did learn the rudiments of the subjects. What a contrast to 21st century primary school education.

In 1948 my father received an invitation to spend six months in New York attached to the unit run by Dr Burrill Crohn in Mount Sinai Hospital. Crohn had described the sometimes-debilitating disease which bears his name also known as regional ileitis. What to do with the two children?

The answer was to leave them with my maternal grandparents in Sheffield. It was arranged that I spend the summer term in 1948 in Westbourne School, a well-regarded institution in the south of the city. At that time my grandparents were still living in Stoke Hall (see below) near Grindleford in Derbyshire some 12 miles away so my grandfather took me to school on the way to his cutlery factory. I remember very little about that term except playing cricket, but I think the education was very satisfactory. My sister who was not quite two years old was looked after by a live-in nanny. She was later dismissed by my grandmother. My grandparents, Emile and Rose Viner, were good fun and had been quite sporty in their younger days, playing tennis, golf and skiing. My grandmother had taken flying lessons before the war but had to stop these on the outbreak of hostilities. They were enthusiastic ballroom dancers and were often first up on the floor when attending a party. Grandpa also fished in the nearby dams which supplied the water for the house.

My great grandmother Jean Herbert (mother of Rose) came to visit for a weekend or so in summer 1948. She was well over eighty and it was reported that when playing cricket with her I exhorted her to run between wickets by shouting 'run Grandma run'. I also have an image of three of my grandfather's brothers coming to Stoke Hall to play bridge.

Stoke Hall, was an imposing three storey Georgian residence, dating in its current form from the middle of the 17th century.

Although it had an entry in the Domesday book the first resident was Gerbert de Stoke early in the 13th century. My grandparents bought the house around 1937 when it was in a dilapidated state. The property was situated on one side of the road to Grindleford backing onto the river Derwent; on the other side of the road was garaging for 3

Stoke Hall, west front, c.1900

cars (previously stables), a flat above these and a large walled garden with greenhouses. At purchase the Hall required significant upgrading and maintenance within the house as well as the property estate.

After completing the summer term at Westbourne School, I was free to roam the countryside and visit the nearby farm with Grandpa's dog, an affectionate chow called Chinky. Political correctness had not surfaced yet. Unfortunately, the summer was marred for my grandparents by a serious car accident when my grandfather's head went through the windscreen when he was being driven to Sheffield at night in a Wolsley. There were no seat belts in those days and this would not have happened after the introduction of mandatory seat belt usage. Glass penetrated one eye and my grandmother raced from home to the hospital to pick fragments of glass from his eye for the rest of the night. He recovered but developed traumatic glaucoma requiring treatment for the rest of his life. The introduction of mandatory seat belt usage is one of the public health triumphs of the 20th century.

In April 1948, my parents sailed to New York and rented a small apartment on the lower East side of Manhattan. They were able to interact with family on my father's side as well as many friends and relatives of my mother's parents so by all accounts they had a good time in post war USA. Many people were strongly advising Dad to remain in the country, but he chose to return to UK.

In late summer, my parents sailed from New York to Southampton on the Cunard liner Mauretania. The day before their arrival my grandmother and I were driven to London to stay with my great grandmother. As a small boy this was very exciting. Grandma Jean lived in a small apartment in Grosvenor square where she had lived right through World War Two, and I remember sleeping in a small box room. That night I had a toffee and a molar tooth stuck to it and fell out. The next day we proceeded to Southampton, and I stood on the quayside gaping in awe at this huge passenger ship. My parents were waving, and we spotted them. After disembarking it became apparent that my mother had been on a buying spree purchasing tinned food, items unavailable in UK at that time because of rationing. Separate transport had to be arranged for these goods, a bit like a camel train! We made our way back to Sheffield and then onto Glasgow where I re-joined the junior school in Glasgow Academy.

CHAPTER 3

School Days

Until I was about eleven, I really did no work in or out of school. The class size was around twenty-eight and I regularly came 25th or so. My main aim in life seemed to be to get home from school as quickly as possible so that I could go out and play. Piano practice was done grudgingly. I was known as Lazy Laz.

Then one year I was revising for exams and asked my mother to test me on the rivers of S. America. It soon became apparent that I was woefully ignorant about these. I suddenly woke up and won 3 prizes at the end of the summer term exams. Other memories about that time included a master who broke a boy's wrist with the belt. I am sure he did not mean to do this but just as the belt was descending the boy moved his wrist. I passed into the senior school still in the B stream but was assigned to the A stream for several subjects and now was placed fourth or fifth in the class. I also managed to pass grade three in piano. During 1954 my parents were discussing whether I should go to public school in England. Two cousins from Sheffield were attending Malvern college and another cousin, also from Sheffield was about to enter Rugby School. On the return journey from Bournemouth where we had been on vacation in summer 1954, we visited Rugby School on the way to Sheffield. It was mid-August, and the school was closed for summer and no prior appointment had been made. The upshot was that I was offered a place contingent on passing common entrance examination.

In November 1954 I celebrated my Barmitzvah which involved reading and singing some extracts from the bible followed by a dinner dance in the main hotel in Glasgow. This was all highly successful as well as enjoyable and my parents and family were proud of me. I certainly received lots of presents. In fact, there were so many fountain pens that I qualified for the well-known phrase 'Today I am a fountain pen'! The same could be said for alarm clocks. Later, I did pass the common entrance exam for Rugby and entered the school in the summer term of 1955 aged thirteen and a half. That term I was placed in an overspill house (Troy) with six other boys from different base houses. Troy happened to be located next to Cotton house which was convenient. I was in the lowest class during this term but settled well and found the work relatively easy. Normally, pupils stayed in that form for at least two if not three terms but I was promoted to the form above for the next year.

By today's standards Rugby school was pretty archaic. We wore one shirt per week with two button down collars and a black tie. The latter was to signify that we were still in mourning for Queen Victoria who died in 1901! The bathing facilities in most houses were primitive. In my case they consisted of a circular steel tub so that it was impossible to lie straight out. In addition, we were only allowed three baths per week. We were encouraged to wash our feet every night in one of the washbasins attached to the dormitory and there were random foot inspections conducted by the prefects. Despite of or because of these privations we were healthy and clean.

The food in my house was sufficient in quantity if occasionally unappetising ranging to inedible. The spending per boy was £1.2s.71/2 d (one pound, two shillings and seven pence ha'penny – approximately £21.50 in 2021). The food situation was supplemented with a 'tuck box' sent from home. It contained chocolate bars, mandarin oranges (tinned) and other delicacies, including refreshments and non-alcoholic drinks. Having said all that, the teaching was good and the class sizes around sixteen -twenty . Homework (prep) was done after supper in the house. The boys were from varied backgrounds but basically middle class. There were about twenty-twenty five Jewish boys in the school out of around seven hundred. In my house there were around sixty boys of whom three or four were Jewish; we did not go to school chapel in the morning but did attend a Jewish service on Sunday attended by all the Jewish boys in the school and conducted by a reform Rabbi who travelled up from London. Remarks addressed to me of an anti-Semitic nature were quite frequent but gradually subsided and I was never physically attacked. I believe, for the most part, that these remarks were made out of ignorance; schoolboys do not like any physical or behavioural characteristic that is outside from their normal experience. Gradually, as I stood up to them, these comments and insults became less frequent and I was accepted for what I was. I have to say however that the nastier incidents did leave some permanent scars.

A year following my school entrance, in June 1956, a happy event occurred. I had been out with my friends but on my return was called to the housemaster's study to be told that I had a new baby sister and that both mother and baby were doing well. Michele had arrived! I was to see her first when she was around one month old and she seemed very content.

Meanwhile my academic studies were going well. I sat O levels (modern GCSEs) in May/June 1957 when I was fifteen and a half and passed all 8 subjects. There were no grades apart from pass/fail. I had to then decide on my A level choices. Although I liked history, I thought it best to study for a possible medical career and opted for Chemistry, Physics and Biology when I entered the sixth form. At this point I enjoyed school more and more. I reached and attained grade 3 in piano. I was in the house rugby team usually at right wing (as I was quite a fast sprinter) and participated in many sports (eg Javelin throwing) on sports day in the summer.

Cotton House Rugby XV 1958. I am seated at far left (middle row).

I also appeared in one house play. I was quite a sociable young man, in particular, friendly with 3 other boys in my house. Three of us subsequently became medical doctors and we all went around together at school. The fourth member of our group studied accountancy after 3 years at New College Oxford. It turned out that he was gay and died from AIDS in his forties. When parents came down at weekends each of us often invited one or more to lunch.

I only saw my parents about once per term which was the normal expectation; I also saw my grandparents from Sheffield as well. I did write a letter almost every week to my parents and my mother wrote back. Every so often I received a letter from my father, often indecipherable as doctors are. A number of young ladies were also in touch by post and their mail was eagerly awaited!

In addition to the standard sports, I started fencing which I enjoyed at school and as a medical student. I played tennis to a reasonable level and managed to win the school doubles while in the 5th form. I enjoyed playing rugby football in the autumn term. I continued to play wing three quarter as I was very fast. However, my tackling skills were not of the best, a point made on one of my reports at the end of term. I also took a woodworking course and studied American history as an 'option' in the sixth form. On entering the sixth form I became a prefect and enjoyed some privileges such as being allowed toast! I also occupied a single study after many years of sharing with one other.

It was suggested to me that I might try to gain entrance to Oxford or Cambridge to study medicine. I discovered that the A level standard was broadly equivalent to the first year in Glasgow University so that if I had entered that institution in 1959, I could have graduated in 1964 assuming I would be given entry to the second year. The alternative was to enter Oxford or Cambridge in 1960. Then the six year course would see me a graduate in 1966. I sought to reduce this date by sitting the entrance exam for University College Oxford to enter in 1959 but, following interview, was not offered a place. In retrospect this was a good outcome as I was offered a place at Queens' College Cambridge starting in October 1960. The interview was mainly with Dr Max Bull, the senior tutor who was an anatomist. It was fairly informal and I suspect he had received appropriate information from my school. I knew a little about this college as my cousin Roger Viner (who had been at Malvern college) was due to come down from Queens' in 1959. I passed the three A levels that I sat in June 1959 and performed well enough in Chemistry to attain scholarship level. The marks in Biology and Physics were not so impressive but I passed. I then went back to school for the third-year 6th form for one term mainly to study for the 4th MB part one in organic chemistry which was required by Cambridge to enter medical studies. I sat this exam in December 1959 at Cambridge and passed. That was my last term at school. I had really enjoyed the course in this subject. Looking back at my time at Rugby I was immensely privileged to have been there. From a somewhat faltering start I developed physically, mentally and intellectually. There is no doubt that my entrance to Cambridge was facilitated by the 'old boy network' in that masters at Rugby had connections with tutors at Cambridge and I acknowledge this. However, there were around twelve applications for every place in the medical course, so in the judgement of the tutors must have shown some desirable qualities.

CHAPTER 4

GAP Year

There has been much written about the benefits of a 'gap year' between school and University. My gap year was approximately ten months, and I was truly fortunate and privileged in that the first 3 months I spent at home in Glasgow working in a stockbroker's office as a junior. I was paid £2 10 shillings per week plus luncheon vouchers. Basically, I was the message boy who transported share certificates and other confidential documents to and from the Glasgow Stock exchange and other stockbroker offices. It is hard to think of this now but there was no fax, no computer and only a slow ticker tape and land line, a far cry from the instant communication of today. I learnt a bit about commerce and the stock market and attended night classes on Strindberg.

In April 1960 I moved to Sheffield and lived with my grandparents while having a job in Viners Ltd, a company founded by my grandfather and his brother Adolph in the early 20th century. Viners was the largest cutlery and hollowware company in the UK with around a thousand employees and I was initially assigned to the packing department. Later, I was asked to help reconcile some accounts in a firm located in the very centre of Sheffield which Viners had recently acquired. This firm, Harrison Brothers and Howson, was a very high-quality cutlery firm producing goods for Harrods and other high end retail outlets. However, it grew to be very inefficient and was heading for insolvency. The property was its main asset. My period in Sheffield was very rewarding as I met several relatives (all from the Viner family) and the social life was good as well. I mostly mixed with the small Jewish community there and was just entering a relationship when I departed for USA.

Emile and Rose Viner in the 1930s
(Note cigarettes being smoked by both!)

When I was in Glasgow in early 1960 a visiting pathologist, Professor Stanley Robbins, arrived from Boston to work with Prof Tom Symington in his department of pathology at Glasgow Royal Infirmary. Robbins came from The Mallory Institute of Pathology attached to Boston City Hospital and was a very experienced pathologist. His textbook of pathology was widely read in many countries. My father, who knew Symington well, befriended Robbins. When he heard that I was going to USA for three months he arranged for me to work at the Mallory, specifically to participate in the pregnancy testing service during the summer period. This was an exciting venture for an 18-year-old just out of school and not having started the medical course in UK. I hastened back to Glasgow to obtain the necessary visa qualifications to work in the USA. As I was going to earn around $100 per week, I required an immigration visa which involved having a Chest X-ray showing no evidence of tuberculosis and a blood test for syphilis! I was pleased to note that both these tests were negative. Nevertheless, I was required to present the X-ray on entering the US customs in New York as well as the signed confirmation relating to the other test.

I boarded The Queen Mary in Southampton for the trip to New York. I had a tourist class ticket and shared a cabin in the bowels of the vessel with 3 other people I did not know. We set sail on Thursday 26th May 1960. The Queen Mary was a huge ship and there were plenty of activities to benefit from even in tourist class. We could also lie out on a lounger and be tucked up with blankets by a steward! It really was life on the ocean wave. After leaving Cherbourg, where we stopped to take on more passengers, we discovered what the Atlantic Ocean was really like. It became so rough that hardly anyone came to the restaurant for breakfast. The sides of the tables were up to prevent items sliding to the floor. The ship rolled alarmingly even though stabilisers had been fitted. After much jollity and around 4 days sailing, we saw The Statue of Liberty near the Hudson River and proceeded to a berth on the west side of Manhattan on Tuesday 31st May. It had been a wonderful experience for me, and I was excited to disembark and meet some family on the quayside.

My father had two first cousins in New York, Muriel Sackler and Sydney Lazarus. They were the children of my paternal grandfather's sibling David. Muriel and two of her three children were waiting for me to disembark; then we all piled into her large red Buick convertible and eventually arrived at her apartment on Riverside Drive on the West side of Manhattan. I was certainly captivated by my first of many visits to New York. The cars streaming up and down Riverside drive, the buzz of Manhattan and of course the number of skyscrapers all made a big impression on me. I was a tourist and next day went to the top of the Empire state building where I met some friends I had made on the Queen Mary. After visiting the UN building, I turned up at The Waldorf Astoria Hotel to meet an acquaintance of my maternal grandfather who lived there! He was a whisky importer who had survived the prohibition as well as the stock market crash of 1929. At dinner that night in The Four Seasons restaurant he introduced me to a US General, a stockbroker and a hotel owner. A good night was had by all.

During the week I went on the floor of Wall Street stock exchange, had lunch at the Rockefeller centre and managed to go to Madison square Garden for a marvellous jazz concert featuring Gene Krupa, Dizzy Gillespie and other great names including Woody Herman and Louis Armstrong. Muriel was divorced from her husband Morty (Mortimer) Sackler father of her three children. In 1960 she was in the middle of studying for a PhD in Biochemisty at Cornell University in Manhattan. She had already obtained a master's degree in Massachusetts Institute of Technology (MIT) in Boston Mass. some years before.

Her parents David and his wife Fanny lived in a modest apartment in Flatbush, Brooklyn and on a Saturday afternoon Muriel lent me her car to go and visit them. It was the classy red Buick. However, I missed the address by a country mile and landed up in Coney Island! Fortunately, I recovered and found my way there eventually. I also met with Sydney and Esther who I had encountered in Glasgow when they were visiting and who were so helpful when we came to live in New York around fifteen years later. Sydney had actually attended a Glasgow medical college for the early part of his medical degree as there was a quota in force in many medical schools on the Eastern seaboard regarding the admission of Jewish students. When WW2 broke out, he left for Switzerland and subsequently completed his medical studies back in USA at The University of Chicago.

I had certainly packed in a lot of experience for a first visit to New York in a short time.

I then took a bus from NYC to Springfield Massachusetts (about 80 miles west of Boston) where some of the Wiener family lived. They had not changed their name to Viner, and I met a first cousin of my grandfather (Amelia Stone married to Jack). It turned out there were many relatives living in the town and their ancestors had been there since the 1880s. In fact, at that time there were 3 brothers who comprised the police force of the town. Subsequently Janet Pilnick (another Wiener relative) took me to her apartment in Boston where I was going to stay during my job at Boston City Hospital (BCH).

This was my first job in a hospital environment. I was to work in the Ascheim-Zondek (AZ) lab., named after two German endocrinologists who practised in the 1930's in Germany but were then forced to leave. Dr Zondek had already written a textbook of endocrinology which was widely read and quoted before he took up residence in Israel. The duties of the lab were to perform pregnancy testing on all women who attended the BCH who requested it.

Unlike today there were no simple tests available from the chemist or pharmacy and the test was not an exact science. It consisted of the injection of maternal urine into the dorsal (rear) sac of a male frog. After a period the urine of the frog was examined under a microscope and if sperm were present the test was positive. It was a true 'end organ effect'. The technician in the lab was Frances a large very pleasant, black lady who taught me what to do and become sufficiently proficient so that she could go on holiday for two weeks. The frogs arrived as a weekly shipment from Madison Wisconsin; unpacking them sometimes led to escapees but most were caught.

The Mallory Institute of Pathology was a world-famous institute founded by Dr Mallory and his son, also Dr Mallory who was still working on the staff. One event really caught my attention, the neuropathology session. The lecture theatre was packed: the resident (then equivalent to the British senior registrar) presented the case history and then came the denouement. The brain had been kept for six weeks in order to make it firm enough to slice through. An air of expectancy and tension was almost palpable in the audience. The junior neuropathologist started the sectioning and the consultant(s) would comment appropriately (remember there were no CT scans or MRI). Of course, as a pre-med student I did not understand everything but the performance was certainly memorable.

I befriended a medical student (Burton Golub) who was in his 3rd year at MIT and who also lived in Brookline where I was. He was bright, quite cynical and good fun. Burt introduced me to many of his friends in Boston which ensured I had a very sociable time. During the summer we went to several beach parties which were very entertaining. Eventually Frances took her vacation, and I was left on my own to run the pregnancy testing service for Boston

City Hospital and managed to do this without any serious problems. During my time in Massachusetts, I managed to visit several relatives on my mother's side (Wieners) and also on my father's side. I also visited many museums in Boston and realised what a marvellous city it was and still is, medically and culturally. Janet, whose smart duplex I was staying in, located in Brookline near Coolidge corner, was a relative and grew up in Kansas City. She ran a high class fashion dress shop on Brookline Avenue and made trips every so often to the garment district in 7th Ave NYC to buy the latest couture. Sadly, her husband had died a few years before and I never met him. He had a long history of diabetes. Janet smoked incessantly and was thin and somewhat 'nervy'. She was very generous to me and took me to her club in Boston and to meet and eat with her friends and married niece and also to Springfield once or twice. I shall be forever grateful to her.

On 31st July, after completing my duties at BCH, I set off in my car to see some country, visit relatives and contacts and have a holiday. I do not think an 18-year-old would be allowed to do this on their own today. I drove to Toronto to stay with Ben Geneen, a psychiatrist from Glasgow, his wife Pearley, a cousin through the Woolfson lineage and their 2 children, Lucy and her brother, David. Detroit and Chicago were next where I visited art museums in the latter and first came across the work of Charles Rennie Mackintosh (although he came from Glasgow!). I also went to the famous stockyards on the south side which was exciting. I continued to Indianapolis and Washington DC staying in motels or with cousins. After Washington I spent a couple of nights in Westport Connecticut and then back to Springfield MA where I sold the car back to Jack for $30! (It only cost $100). The car had performed very well during the last 3 weeks and approximately three thousand miles although it did need new tires and a muffler (exhaust). I learnt a huge amount during this vacation – firstly about people some quite modest in their income, others very wealthy. They were all very kind and hospitable. Secondly, I was able to gain an impression of other American cities as well as the countryside although I realised that this experience only was a fraction of USA. Thirdly I was encouraged that I made the trip on my own and was resilient enough to have done so. Eventually I took the train to New York and had time over a few days to see some people before boarding the ship to Liverpool. Again, the transatlantic crossing was very sociable, and the sea was not so rough as on the outgoing journey. The ship docked in Liverpool from where I travelled to Sheffield, then staying a few days before travelling back to Glasgow.

I am sure that after this year it will come as no surprise that I strongly recommend a gap year for prospective university students. I was able to experience aspects of commerce, finance and medicine as well as earning some wages in each of the three jobs I had. I must thank my parents, grandparents and everyone in USA for supporting me, especially Muriel Sackler (as she was then) and Janet Pilnick.

CHAPTER 5

University of Cambridge

I arrived in Cambridge in October 1960 to read Natural Sciences Tripos part I. It was very stimulating to be in the company of so many other students at my college (Queens') as well as other people from school in different colleges who were also studying for medicine. I soon discovered that the Cambridge experience was a long way up from school (even a good one). You were left to your own devices in terms of how much work you did. There were no set books although obviously you were expected to be acquainting yourself with the subject. In general, lectures were not compulsory but given that they were delivered by world class scientists (not necessarily high-class lecturers) they were worth attending. I particularly enjoyed the biochemistry lectures as they were very up to date drawing on findings discovered by Cambridge scientists as well as others. At that time advances in molecular biology and structural biology were taking place in Cambridge but most students had no idea about these developments. They resulted in the acquisition of Nobel prizes awarded to several scientists whose work is described in a book by the late Sir John Meurig Thomas (Architects of Structural Biology, 2020, Oxford University Press).

The biochemistry course was so good that I attended the lectures 2 years running. The physical domain of the lecture theatre encouraged the use of marbles as the stairs up to the top were quite steep and even the noise of one accelerating marble was loud especially when accompanied by the increasing cheers of the students! Several marbles amplified the experience for all of us. The rhythmic clapping of the student body got faster and faster, sometimes quick enough to put off even the most experienced lecturer, or so we thought. I would be the first to admit that this was childish behaviour.

An amusing incident, also at Cambridge concerned a physiology lecturer who was a short slight gentleman. At the front of the lecture theatre there were long roller blackboards which could be raised electronically once full to bring the next one into view. On pushing up the blackboard the lecturer, for some reason, kept hold of the handles and he started to lift off from the ground. As if that was not enough his knees made contact with some other buttons on the control panel which caused the electric blinds to descend and at the same time the lights went out. The ensuing student uproar, banging desks and cheering was a sight to behold! Order was eventually restored but the incident was never forgotten.

A distinctive feature of the learning experience was the supervision system which was the main driver to work. In each subject (Anatomy, Physiology and Biochemistry) groups of 4 or 5 attended a supervision given by a college member. We were required to write an essay each week in each subject, and I (mostly) performed this with enthusiasm. The supervisor marked these assiduously and the comments were very helpful. The anatomy tutor was Dr Bull who was the senior tutor and a very kindly man. He had a twinkle in his eye. On one occasion when we were asked to describe the anatomy of the female breast my co student Malcom Read made some error in the description of the distance between the two resulting in Max (Bull) commenting 'It's only a gutter Read not an arterial road'. Bull was a superb anatomist and lectured on embryology on a Saturday morning. Most of us were the worse for wear at this time of the week and I never got to grips with intricacies of this branch of anatomy. Max was a father figure to all the medical students in Queens' and could relax with them; for example, at the annual Queens' College Medical Society dinner he was to be seen standing on a chair conducting many of us (mostly inebriated) in a rendering of 4 and 20 blackbirds.

The Natural Sciences Tripos part I could be completed in 2 or 3 years. If a second-class degree or above was obtained this ensured admission to a medical school, usually in London. For clinical studies in those days, there was no clinical school at Cambridge so another choice for clinical studies was imperative. If the part I was completed in 2 years the student could undertake a part II in any subject of his/her choosing. I chose to complete part I in 2 years and also to apply to Glasgow University Medical School to complete medical studies after my 3rd year at Cambridge. I was interviewed in Glasgow and while I was accepted for the course starting in the fourth year, I was told that Glasgow University did not recognise the BA degree as a qualification to enter the medical curriculum! I was amazed by this. I therefore had to sit the 2nd MB professional examination in Glasgow during the term I was completing the part I in Cambridge and I duly flew up from London during the Lent term to do this. In fact, I sat this exam with the year ahead of me in Glasgow and was admitted to the University the following autumn (in 1963).

Meanwhile back in Cambridge I passed the tripos exam in summer 1962 and had been accepted to enter the Experimental psychology course for my part II. I had been interviewed by the head of department Prof OL Zangwill and indicated that I wanted to be a neurologist hence this course would be very suitable. In view of the fact that I had already gained a place in medicine following Cambridge and that the class of the BA degree was that obtained in the part I I slacked off somewhat during the psychology course. I remember having to produce 1 essay per week and perform 1 practical class per week. In retrospect I should have worked harder. There were courses in Physiological psychology, experimental psychology, educational and industrial psychology and more, all given by acknowledged experts in their field. Meanwhile I was enjoying fencing, socialising, and appreciating the delights of Cambridge. It was therefore not very surprising that I was awarded only a 3rd class degree in psychology at the end of the year but fortunately this did not affect my overall second-class degree.

The long vacation after the summer term offered a chance for everyone to do something exciting. My first long vac (as it was called) in 1961 we first had to go up to Cambridge to do some more anatomy. Not so exciting you might think. Indeed, but this is when all the foreign language schools opened for English courses and many continental girls were looking for men in addition to learning English. Much socialising and many opportunities but no long-term relationship for me.

At the end of this 5-week period, I was part of a 5 man expedition to The Soviet Union. We had bought an old baker's van and put in a back seat. The van was a gear shift, had done around 80,000 miles and had good storage. Jonathan Dowson and I were the 2 medics in addition to an engineer, a classics student who knew Cyrillic and a modern language student. The van would not do more than 45 mph; however, we arrived in Moscow via Berlin. The Berlin wall was erected in August 1961 just after we had driven through West and East Berlin and then Poland before arriving in Moscow. Most of the time we were camping and eating our own provisions. Our eyes were opened to the serious poverty in the East. There were few cars and petrol stations were only every 200 miles with manual pumps. Shops were also few and far between with a limited range of goods for sale. There was evident poverty in the countryside. After spending time in Moscow seeing sights and trading on the black market (mostly in socks and miniatures of Scotch whisky), we bought fur hats and vinyl records in GUM, the large state-owned store situated in Red Square. We were camping in a suburb of Moscow as were several other groups of tourists. One group of Americans took the black market very seriously and went out in the morning to do business. They returned eventually with no clothes on except their underwear and raincoats with roubles stuffed into the pockets! We visited the lying in state of Lenin and Stalin also in the same location in Red Square.

Finally, we set off for Leningrad, as it was named then, stopping at Kalinin and Novgorod on the way. The sightseeing at Leningrad was spectacular and the intourist guide was highly informative. After 2 or 3 days of incessant culture including the Hermitage Museum we departed for the Finnish border. Arriving in Finland was like a transformation. For example, we saw an Esso petrol sign! It made us realise what an enormous difference in living standard there was between countries controlled by The Soviet Union and the West. It took another 28 years before the Berlin wall came down and some developments in democracy appeared in countries behind the iron curtain. In that interval the west had witnessed brutal suppression of uprisings in Prague and Budapest in addition to draconian regulations relating to emigration from Soviet Union and other countries, particularly Berlin in Germany. Escape to the west by Rudolph Nureyev, Vladimir Ashkenazi and others featured prominently in western newspapers and must have infuriated the Soviet administration. Going behind the iron curtain was the highlight of our trip although the return journey through Finland, Sweden, Denmark, Germany, and The Netherlands also very informative with many museums to visit. Back in England from Belgium we realised we had been abroad for just under 7 weeks and had motored for very nearly 5000 miles, not bad for an old baker's van! As a group we had bonded well together, seen a lot of sights and appreciated different cultures. It was an exhilarating holiday.

A feature of both Cambridge and Oxford is the short term-time of only about 8 weeks. The result is that work is very concentrated, and play is also hard. This is a good recipe for energetic students as it leaves plenty of time during the vacations. In the summer vacation of 1962, the medics again had to attend for a 'long vac term' to dissect head and neck but we had a great social life as well with no imminent exams. I had arranged a job in the Dept of physiology in the medical school in Jerusalem for the rest of the vacation and this was certainly an adventure. In July I travelled from London to Athens by train sharing the compartment with the local population including geese in former Yugoslavia. Arriving in Athens near midnight I did not have any accommodation but managed to share a room with a fellow traveller. I boarded a ship next day and eventually arrived in Jerusalem.

The posting was supported by the professional and technical workers association (PATWA), an initiative from the Israeli government to attract eventual immigration. My lodgings were in the flat of a lady whose husband was in Argentina as a diplomat and there was another medical student from USA. He was Jay Levy who went on to be a distinguished viral immunologist especially in the field of HIV. The flat was located very centrally near the King David Hotel. More importantly it was near the physiology laboratory which was located on the border of the then divided city. Most of the rest of the medical school was in Ein Karem hospital complex on the outskirts of the city. In the lab I was attached to a British scientist who was working on oxygen utilisation of the brain. Cecil Allweiss was familiar with isotope work and had spent time with the famous scientist I L Chaikoff in California. The model we used was the dog and after injection of radioactive glucose the sagittal sinus (the main vein in the top of the head) was canulated to collect samples. The dog was, of course, anaesthetised and put down after the day long experiment. The department was large with other workers involved in research mostly to do with neurophysiology. As the lab was right on the border of East Jerusalem gunfire was often heard which was rather alarming, at least to me.

I had several contacts in Israel. One of them was Professor Isaac Michaelson, Professor of Ophthalmology in Jerusalem University. He was from Glasgow and was coping with a large number of patients as well as writing a definitive textbook on his subject. At that time The Soviet Union was allowing Jewish emigration from Russia to Israel. There was a Russian ship due to arrive in Haifa with 1000 blind people on board and Michaelson had to supervise their assessment and placement. This was how The Soviet Union prioritised its emigration strategy. I managed to visit many areas of the country as well as experiencing a couple of nights on a kibbutz and help with the crop harvesting. I slept on the beach in Eilat as well as hiking in the north.

My cousin Linda and her (then) boyfriend Mark (now married more than 50 years) had a car and were very kind to include me in various trips. The main excursion was for Mark and I to motor back to Glasgow. We started by taking a ferry from Haifa to Izmir (Turkey) and then began an eventful and exciting journey through part of the iron curtain countries, central Europe and on to Holland. We stayed with Mark's grandmother in Antwerp for a night before boarding a ferry to England.

My second year in Cambridge was mostly taken up with work, learning to cox an eight at rowing on the Cam and socialising. I also found time to notice and appreciate aspects of life peculiar to Cambridge. In late Autumn returning to college in the increasing gloom of a Sunday afternoon the sound of bells ringing from different churches was quite moving. Similar emotions in another context were provided by the madrigal singing in a summer evening on the Cam. A line of punts would process along the river with the leading one containing the madrigal singers. As it got dark, candles were lit in this punt and the singing started. In the following punts moderate amounts of wine were consumed which perhaps added to the appreciation of this genre of music.

I found physiology and biochemistry easy but had to spend an inordinate amount of time learning anatomy. By the end of the year, I knew Gray's Anatomy almost by heart. I gained entrance to the clinical part of the medical course in Glasgow starting in October 1963. Early 1962 was the coldest winter for many years. The East of England received icy blasts straight from the Steppes of Russia. As well as this we had copious amounts of snow and the country nearly ground to a halt. In Cambridge the river Cam froze and we were able to skate all the way to Grantchester (about 3 miles). In the college the gas supply froze so we could not toast our crumpets! and everything was a bit fraught. In the summer term I worked really hard revising for the part I of the Natural sciences tripos which I sat in May. Although I

My parents Sam and Thelma Lazarus in 1960's

performed well in physiology my overall degree was 2.2 but this was enough to allow me to enter the clinical part of the course elsewhere.

I was elected as president of The Queens' College Medical Society and enjoyed chairing the monthly meetings with speakers who I had largely chosen. Although I also appreciated the psychology course I only achieved a third class degree at the end but the experience stood me in good stead later in my research career. Looking back at my 3 years in Cambridge I would say they were transformative. You were treated as an adult for better or for worse. I learnt how to think and met a wide variety of extremely bright students and teachers. My fellow medics and I from Queens' were competent but not brilliant, apart from 2 who went on to attain 1st class degrees. However, we all had something to contribute to life, sports, and friendship. In fact, we were a very close-knit group and after going down from Cambridge formed a club that has met every year for a dinner. This takes place one year at Queens' and one year outside Cambridge. To everyone's amazement this has now been going for 60 years with only one break due to the Covid pandemic and is enjoyed by all. Graduating BA in Cambridge in June 1963 was a memorable experience for a 21-year-old. The ceremony took place in the Senate House and we wore the appropriate gowns. My parents came down from Glasgow as well as my sister Suzanne. My mother's parents also came and enjoyed the ceremony and the whole family seemed proud of their son's (grandson's) achievement. My grandparents had moved to Bournemouth from Sheffield, and I accompanied them home to spend a day or two before returning to Glasgow. The whole Cambridge experience is one I look back on with immense pleasure. It was a privilege to meet a variety of colleagues and be exposed to world class scientists.

In the long vacation that followed I attended Addenbrookes Hospital for an Introductory course in Medicine. This was really exciting as we saw real (and some extremely sick) patients. Following this I had decided to return to the lab in Jerusalem to continue the perfusion studies started in 1962 I flew to Israel via Cyprus and immersed myself in the dog brain. I lived in a room in Rehavia, a good suburb not too far from the lab and spent an enjoyable 2 months or so in research and more travelling within Israel. My spoken Hebrew even improved a bit. Unfortunately, the research never really came to a meaningful conclusion and no academic paper was written. Nevertheless, I benefitted from working in a lab and the interaction with other scientists. I began to realise that research work was not easy and there were frequent disappointments; perseverance was critically important.

CHAPTER 6

University of Glasgow

Returning to Glasgow I joined the 4th year of Glasgow University medical school and started my exposure to clinical medicine in earnest. There was (and still is) only one medical school in a city of around a million inhabitants and many hospitals. Our days were organised and we were expected to attend all lectures and clinical work. The former were in Pathology and Materia Medica (Pharmacology and Therapeutics) and my first clinical experience was in the Professorial medical unit in the Western infirmary. Each day was devoted to a different body system (eg. cardiac, respiratory etc). It soon became apparent to me that learning to examine a patient was not easy. Basically, there are three steps, taking a history, performing a physical examination and, based on the results of information gained, arranging appropriate tests if necessary. Often a diagnosis may be arrived at after the history and examination. Sometimes, even after testing the blood and other procedures the diagnosis is still not clear, but a provisional diagnosis should be entered in the patient's case notes. We attended in groups of about 5-7and the consultants took their role very seriously together with the junior staff. Patients were often earmarked the day before as being suitable and their permission sought. We were also taught how to present the case to the clinician and to use appropriate language when discussing the findings with the patient. It is hard to believe but many terms (eg. cancer, tuberculosis etc) were considered too forthright to mention to or in front of a patient. We were given a booklet indicating patient friendly terms or phrases (eg. mitotic lesion, lump, acid fast bacilli etc). Of course today one has to explain the disease clearly and frankly to the patient.

After the first clinical year students were encouraged to do an elective project. Normally this was done during the summer usually out of Glasgow and often abroad. I had the opportunity to work in The Truesdale Hospital a small (two hundred bed) hospital in Fall River Mass. USA, about 60 miles south of Boston. The job consisted of 2- or 3-week rotations through many specialities and helping out as much as possible. It was a good opportunity for me to improve my clinical examination skills in addition to observing many consultants in their everyday practice. Although small, the standard of medicine was very high. In fact, one of the physicians subsequently became dean of Brown University medical school in Rhode Island. One of the surgeons took myself and another member of my Glasgow year to the Grand rounds in surgery in The Massachusetts General Hospital in Boston. This was and still is a world-famous facility, so it was very stimulating to enter the Bigelow theatre where the round was held.

Fall River was a small city and famous as the place where Lizzie Borden participated in the so-called Fall River cult murders. The authorities in the city heard that we (Jayne Aitken and I) were working as externs in the hospital. They asked us to an evening in a public hall where we were invited to speak about life in Glasgow and the medical care facilities using the National Health Service. We did this to the best of our ability and our photographs duly appeared in the local paper. The whole experience in Fall River was very educational and the staff were very helpful. My clinical examination of patients improved hugely and I felt much more confident.

CHAPTER 7

Glasgow Clinical Sudies

Returning to Glasgow we now started to work towards the final exams in Medicine. A lot of ground had to be covered. At that time Glasgow had a population of around 1 million and the medical school used every type of hospital. There was an infectious disease hospital with high walls round it! In addition to hospital provision for the main subjects (Medicine, Surgery, Child health and Obstetrics and Gynaecology) situated in the West, East, North and South of the city there were separate hospitals for Ear Nose and Throat and Eyes. This resulted in plenty of exposure to patients as a student accompanied by enthusiastic teaching. A consequence of the vast provision of clinical cases was that students were able to appreciate the range of social deprivation in Glasgow at that time. All students were expected to join the obstetric flying squad and I remember visiting one flat which was nothing but bare boards and minimal furniture with a young woman in initial stages of labour and bleeding inappropriately.

My fellow students were genuinely nice to me especially considering that I was the only student to join them in the year. Whether the fact that my father was on the staff of one of the general hospitals made any difference I do not know! Moreover 2 lady students in the year also had fathers on the staff in different hospitals and one of them had been in the same year as my father. Sometimes I found it quite embarrassing to have one's father also a physician in the city. There was quite a lot of 'It's Sam's son'. There were 33% women in the year, a very acceptable number for 60 years ago.

There was a strong group culture in the year with the aim of raising money for the final yearbook and final year dinner. The club was known as The Zeta Club and is alive even today. Dances were held as well as jumble sales, bazaars and other events. The final yearbook consisted of pictures of everyone in the year with suitable accompanying quotes. In addition, it also supported the final year dinner which was held in the January of eventual graduation in June. We have attended several reunions of the year held over 2 days in various locations and hotels near Glasgow. These have been most enjoyable, and it is interesting to see what branch of medicine everyone has followed. More recently, of course, the numbers attending has been less due to quite a high loss rate. I often wonder who is going to be the last person standing!

I had a car which I had bought just after graduating in Cambridge and was still living at home. This was invaluable as we often had to cross the city to attend at different hospitals. I was not the only one so we were able to transport fellow students. From a demographic point of view most of the students came from Glasgow and environs although a substantial minority were from Africa (mainly Nigeria). Glasgow was proud (and still is) to have educated this group most of whom returned to their mother country where medical facilities would vary enormously.

At the end of each term, we had a clinical exam and at the end of the year we sat a professional exam. If you failed the latter, it might mean repeating the entire year. Over the course of the 3 years these exams included pathology and microbiology, Materia medica, public health and medical jurisprudence. Glasgow was famous for its high and tragic murder rate, so the medical jurisprudence course was exceptionally well attended. I well remember the professor lecturing not long after commencement of the course when many female students fainted at the gory slides presented. Passing all these exams allowed entrance to the final year where you were treated as a resident (houseman). This meant that you were attached to a clinical firm as an 'intensive' student with only one or two other final year students for about 3 months and expected to help the resident with his/her duties as well as receive clinical teaching. The last intensive attachment I had was in internal medicine attached to the professorial unit with Prof Sir Edward Wayne.

During the final year I became the editor of Surgo, the medical student magazine. This involved soliciting articles and arranging them on the pages which by today's standard is archaic. There were 3 issues per year, so I was always on the go with this commitment. During this time the final year dinner was held. I am ashamed to admit that there was one dinner for men and a separate one for women, such was the custom of the day. The men's dinner was the culmination of our efforts to raise enough funding to produce the final yearbook. This comprised of quotes gathered over the year for the staff and pictures and quotes for members of the year (men and women!). Many members of staff also attended this dinner and it was a memorable occasion, not least because 1 bottle of whisky was distributed amongst every 4 students to be consumed after the meal. The honorary president of the year Professor Andrew Watt Kay (later Sir Andrew) attended. He was a distinguished surgeon who acted as a role model for many in the year who later trained in surgery. My father who had attended many of these dinners came to this one but went home at a respectable time unlike myself.

There were only two of us final year (intensive) students in Wayne's unit and we both managed to obtain a first class certificate after the clinical examination. To celebrate this my colleague (Martin McKenzie) and I decided that we would visit a local hostelry (The Rubaiyat) for a drink at lunchtime. There were a few ladies there one of whom I later married! So, I was glad I did well in the exam.

The final examinations for the degree of MB ChB were held over 3 weeks in June and in addition to examination papers in medicine, surgery, obstetrics and gynaecology and paediatric medicine and surgery there were clinical examinations in all of these subjects. The latter were held in different hospitals, and it was a triumph of navigation to arrive at the correct hospital at the appointed time. The medical curriculum and examination procedures have changed significantly since those days but both were approved by the General Medical Council as fit for purpose. On the night, the results were published, many of us gathered in groups in different flats and houses to wait nervously. The Glasgow Herald actually published the results so one member of each group was deputed to go down to the printer's office of that newspaper at midnight and return with a copy. I passed!

Four of us subsequently spent 2 weeks in Majorca to celebrate. Memories of this period are now clouded as copious amount of Sangria were consumed. Looking back on my 6 years of medical education I was privileged to have many great learning experiences, meet many new friends, and mature as a person. I will be forever grateful to my teachers, clinical and non- clinical, for their support and encouragement.

CHAPTER 8

Residencies (House Jobs)

I had obtained a residency (house job) in Sir Edward Wayne's unit and started on 1st August 1966. That day there were patients right down the middle of the ward as well as each side (something unheard of today) due to a very busy emergency intake the day before. The outgoing resident merely said we've been very busy, best of luck. So began 6 months of very hard, often sleep deprived work. On that unit there were 4 consultants, a host of junior staff and research fellows and 2 of us residents. We got on very well together to ensure that we survived with little sleep and long working hours. At least you did not have to attend the outpatient clinic as a resident but when I was on the staff after the residency, I did 3 clinics per week.

In the department there were 4 teams relating to Endocrinology, Haematology, Cardiology and Gastroenterology. They were each staffed by a consultant and 3 junior staff. There was also a separate metabolic ward used for special patients including members of staff and the like. As a resident (houseman) we worked for one firm on alternate weekdays and the other on the other days including Saturday morning.

When I was on the staff after the residency, I did 3 or 4 outpatient clinics per week. It was during this time that I learnt how to delegate appropriate tasks to those staff below me and take on more responsibility for patient management. We never counted the hours we worked in a week, and I recognise they were a lot more than those required by current regulations.

My co- resident was a delightful person and we integrated very well. After 3 months we swapped around and this afforded us experience of different specialties and different ways of working. We were resident in hospital which included board and lodging and many parties. A short break was allowed, and a final year student did the locum, again not allowed today. During my time there I remember being asked to take 50ml of blood from certain patients as the junior staff wished to have most of it for research purposes. One large syringe was produced and I duly extracted the blood. I was curious as to the use of this large sample and was then supplied with several papers on the thyroid research that was ongoing in the department. This was the start of my career in endocrinology, in particular, thyroid disease and physiology. I was becoming a thyroid man.

During the 1st 6 months of my residency, I learnt a lot of general medicine as well as appreciating how the hospital functioned overall. Sir Edward Wayne, the Regius professor of Medicine, was awarded his knighthood for chairing the committee which set the upper legal blood level of alcohol for vehicle drivers in the UK and had studied Chemistry before medicine. This gave him an analytical approach to the study of iodine metabolism for which the department was famous. I duly rotated through the other half of the clinical service which comprised cardiology and haematology both groups being staffed by experts in both clinical and research areas.

Christmas time on the wards was great fun. I had to dress up as a woman and go round every male patient giving them a small gift (not to mention a well planted kiss). My co resident had to do the same thing in the female ward. The whole department also went to a local hotel where a Xmas pantomime was performed. I do not really think I suited the blond wig I wore!

During the last 2 months of that job the male ward was being redecorated and we were removed to an old TB hospital in the west of Glasgow. This was good in that we were given more responsibility, and the pace was not so frenetic. I took a day off to travel to Cambridge to sit the MB BChir exam which I passed and thus obtained two medical degrees.

After the 6 month period was completed, I moved to Glasgow Royal Infirmary on the east side of Glasgow. This was also a famous teaching hospital where Joseph Lister had first used carbolic acid to save a young boy who had broken a leg and who otherwise would have died of sepsis. I was attached to a general surgeon with a special interest in chest surgery, a gruff honest Scotsman. There were 3 consultants on the 'flat' and my co resident was a delightful woman (Celia Campbell). We rotated doing 3 months general surgery, 6 weeks Ear Nose and Throat and 6 weeks casualty. All were very good providing plenty of hands-on experience. The casualty job was particularly memorable as at the time (1967) the gang riots in Glasgow were still occurring albeit at a lesser intensity than earlier in the decade. Nevertheless, Monday night was usually simple stabbing but by Friday it was hatchet in the head. Fortunately, there were no gun injuries but plenty of razor slashing often for no apparent reason. The casualty department, known as the gatehouse, was the busiest in Europe in those days but we worked an 8 hour shift and then we were off till the next 24-hour period. Of course, alcohol intoxication was a constant background to many of the trauma cases so much so that, on occasions when we were extremely busy, we did not administer any local anaesthetic before stitching up wounds. Often there were many policemen in the unit restraining the patients while they were dealt with.

By this time, I had decided I did not want to pursue a career in surgery and applied for a senior house officer job in Edinburgh in medicine and diabetes. I was not placed on the short list and while this was happening the department of medicine in the Western Infirmary offered me a scholarship in general medicine (Endocrinology). This was the Christina Hansen Scholarship founded in 1944 by the bequest of William Hansen, MB 1896, of Upminster in memory of his mother. Although it sounded very grand the pay was modest but not unreasonable; I received £200 every quarter free of tax, insurance or pension contributions equivalent to around £15500 in 2022. I was responsible to Dr WD (Donald) Alexander, the reader in Medicine and noted thyroid researcher. It was paid to me in 4 instalments with no deductions for tax or national insurance or anything else. This was enough to live on as I was paying only £5/week for a quarter share of a furnished flat in the West end of Glasgow near the hospital.

I took my 2 weeks holiday at the end of my surgical residency in July. By this time, I had been going out with Maureen Miller who I had met in the pub just before finals for a year or so. Her sister had just had a third child and the family were going to holiday in a cottage in Golspie in NE Scotland. I was invited but before going there I decided to have a look at Skye. I was not ready to propose to Maureen yet as my parents did not really approve of me forming a close attachment with a non- Jewish lady. More of this later. On returning to Glasgow, I moved out of my parent's home into a flat in the West end of the city sharing with 3 others, 2 doctors and an engineer. The flat was a high-end apartment and was well furnished and in good repair. We had to keep it that way! As it so happened Maureen had moved out of her parent's home in Helensburgh and was also living in a flat with several other girls not very far away.

Social life in Glasgow was good in those years. The cinema was very popular, and my friends and I still had our boat on Loch Lomond which was great fun. We all got on well in the flat and that was a great boon. We had one party which rather overstepped the mark as there were far more people there than was sensible and the police were summoned. There were no severe after effects except a headache.

In 1968 my sister Suzanne, 5 years younger than me, married Ken Prysor-Jones who she had met when both were up at Oxford. Unfortunately, the marriage did not last but my parents had experienced the first intermarriage amongst their children. I had started my Senior House Officer (SHO) post on 1st August 1967. There were though 3 dark clouds which were part of life experience. At the end of 1968 a first cousin aged 19 was killed in a motor accident. In 1969 my future sister-in-law had surgery for rectal cancer from which she died just before the birth of our 1st daughter in 1971. Her loss was deeply distressing for the whole family. Also, in 1969 a very experienced and well-respected Lecturer (senior registrar) in our department committed suicide following the sudden death of his wife. All these tragedies made a deep impression on me as I was young at the time.

Nevertheless, a joyous occasion for Maureen and I was the celebration of our marriage 2 days before Christmas in 1969. This took place in Manchester as it was there that Maureen underwent a conversion course to Judaism mainly to please my father. The wedding was small but guests from Sheffield were invited as well as relatives from both sides from Glasgow. On return from honeymoon in

Amsterdam we started life in our 3rd floor flat in the West end of Glasgow, within walking distance of the hospital. Maureen was teaching in a primary school in a rough part of Glasgow with bars on lower floor windows (she received danger money for this employment)! The following year after a holiday in Spain Maureen became pregnant and our first daughter, Tracey was born in May 1971. Very sadly Maureen's sister Pat died 2 weeks before the birth aged 31 leaving her husband, twin boys and a girl. This was a family tragedy but, with a new baby, we had to continue with our lives.

CHAPTER 9

Start of a Medical Career

I arrived in the department of Medicine on August 1st, 1967, as a junior research fellow. In addition to clinical duties and teaching, everyone was encouraged to become involved in research. I was shown a small room as my office in which was a dental chair and a table. The reason for the dental chair soon became apparent. The thyroid team were interested in all aspects of iodine metabolism which of course is the element relating to function of the thyroid gland. The first step in the process of acquisition of iodine by the thyroid gland is concentration of that element from the blood stream. Nowadays there is a huge amount of information on the details of this process but there was really very little information in the 1960's. What was known was that while the thyroid could concentrate iodine to many times the plasma level this ability was also shared by other tissues such as parotid salivary glands. When iodine was taken up by the thyroid it was used in the production of thyroid hormone, but this was not the case in the salivary glands. So, a human experimental model existed for measuring iodine uptake by collecting saliva, hence the dental chair. If a radioisotope of iodine was injected into the subject the radioactivity could be measured in the saliva. A suction cup was applied to the orifice of the salivary gland inside the cheek and a tube attached to this carried the saliva into a glass measuring tube. Also, collection via the tube ensured there was no contamination by saliva secreted from other salivary glands. Different variables could be explored such as time, salivary flow rate and effects of other substances on the concentration of the salivary iodine.

A feature of the department was the involvement of basic non-medical scientists in the research projects. They provided quality control and excellent advice. In the department these scientists were mainly physicists and I shall be forever grateful to Jim Robertson, son of an eminent neurosurgeon, for his cooperation and expertise. We were able to inject not one but several relevant radioisotopes to our subjects and measure relative uptake and other variables. Sadly, Jim passed away a few years ago but we both obtained higher degrees from these studies, an MD for myself and a PhD for Jim.

As well as this core project I became involved in various clinical thyroid studies. I also learnt how to present data at a meeting. The departmental rule was that if you were going to give a presentation you had to rehearse it in front of departmental members. Often, presentations at national meetings were scheduled for 10 minutes together with 5 minutes for discussion. We were only allowed 10 seconds on either side of the 10 minutes! Senior members of the department tried to anticipate the questions; there were also comments on how you were standing. The final result was that if you passed the test, you could deliver a paper anywhere in the world in front of any size of audience. It really was great training.

I soon realised that the priorities in the department were, first, clinical work then teaching and lastly research. These applied whoever you were and whatever seniority. To become a qualified physician, it was necessary to pass the membership exam of the Royal College of Physicians. This was a difficult exam with only a modest pass rate. It was divided into 2 sections; part I was an extensive multiple choice question paper covering all of medicine and part II was a clinical examination associated with a viva voce examination. I passed the part I at the first attempt with a high mark in 1968 and was told I was in the top 10% in the UK but unfortunately failed the part II (clinical) exam on 3 successive occasions after sitting this twice in London and once in Glasgow. This was a severe blow to my confidence and at one point I wondered whether I should leave hospital medicine and try something else. I was determined to have another attempt, but this meant that I was required to sit part I again. I passed this and then passed the clinical exam in Glasgow in 1970. There were potential reasons for the failures but having got married in late 1969 I think that was a positive background factor in aiding the pass.

As a junior doctor in Glasgow, I was involved in looking after patients, after all this is what I had perceived the role of a doctor to be and what we had trained for in medical school. I really enjoyed this aspect of my activities though events proved nerve racking when one had to present a case to colleagues in the Department or in the hospital. Once you had done it once it became a bit easier as you gained confidence. There were also departmental clinical presentations by the different clinical firms which the students were encouraged to attend.

In addition to patient care the members of the department had a duty and responsibility to provide clinical teaching to undergraduate as well as postgraduate students. This task was taken very seriously. For example, junior undergraduates generally had instruction in a different body system every day and the junior doctors were required to arrange a suitable patient (including obtaining permission) the day before. This was made much easier than today as the length of stay of patients in hospital was, on average, much longer.

The most enjoyable part of clinical teaching, at least for me, was the interaction I had with the students when sat round the bedside of a patient in a group of around 6 to 8 to discuss the history of the patient's illness, the physical findings on examination and the possible or probable diagnosis and treatment. Often this also involved discussion of the relevant tests required to investigate or confirm the diagnosis. In view of the amount of time that teaching involved it was not surprising that several departmental members undertook research in this area. However, this sphere of activity was not very popular with the medical hierarchy in the UK at that time who considered it to be a 'soft' area' perhaps with some justification. It was during this time that I learnt how to delegate appropriate tasks to those staff below me and take on more responsibility for patient management. We never counted the hours we worked in a week, and I recognise they were a lot more than those required by current regulations.

In September 1967 Prof Wayne had retired and was succeeded by Prof Graham Wilson, also very interested in thyroid disease. He was very keen that all members should complete an MD thesis. Most theses start with a background chapter reviewing the history of the topic and bringing the reader up to date. Having attained the MRCP certificate the way was now open to planning and working towards my thesis for the MD degree and I started planning on how to achieve this. I spent around 3 months of evenings, mostly on weekdays, in the excellent library of Royal College of Physicians and Surgeons of Glasgow trawling through references to assist me in this first chapter. One evening I read a paper with no references which meant I had arrived at the start point. I also got to know the authors of many of the papers in terms of their progress and movement in working for different research heads mostly in United

States. It was like researching a family tree and I was then able to start my background chapter.

By this time. I was a registrar in the department and active in medical education as well as clinical work and research. One could be opportunistic in those days. An article appeared in the British Medical Journal suggesting that Lithium therapy (administered to patients with bipolar disorder) caused thyroid disturbance leading to goitre. Together with help from my best man (the late) Dr Ernest Bennie, a psychiatrist, we set about investigating this side effect of the drug. I was also continuing the work on salivary gland function and iodine using various isotopes singly and in combination.

Later in 1971 we found that Maureen was pregnant again after a holiday on the Island of Arran. We were still living in the Victorian flat in Glasgow 76 steps up from the street, so it was clear that we had to relocate. A search for a new house started. Meanwhile I had received an offer to go to Nigeria as an SHO to help with teaching medical students and learning some tropical medicine. The offer was from Professor Eldred Parry a well-known worker in the field who died in 2022 aged 91. I discussed this with the head of the department and decided it was too early in my career to take up the offer. Also, in that year I attended my first of very many meetings of The European Thyroid Association which had been founded only a few years before in 1967. I delivered my first communication abroad and was terrified as the audience comprised of many world experts. I had rehearsed the paper in front of the department members at home who were critical where necessary but extremely helpful. I thoroughly enjoyed meeting people from different countries in Europe and hearing different views concerning topics of the day. The meeting was held in Berne, Switzerland and was superbly organised by our Swiss colleagues both academically and socially.

In early 1972 we started searching for new accommodation in earnest but nothing turned up. In May of that year our second daughter, Jennifer (Jenny) arrived on the same date as baby Tracey! Some called it endocrine family planning but not by design! With 2 babies to cope with it was difficult to negotiate the 76 steps but we were very grateful to the occupants of the basement flat for allowing us to park the pram.

During this time, it became apparent to me that there was little chance of promotion within the department or indeed in the Glasgow area and I started applying for posts elsewhere. The first was a lecturer post in Aberdeen and I was called for interview in June 1971. When I stepped off the train, I noticed 2 things; it was freezing cold and the smell of fish was everywhere! I was relieved not to be appointed. I then went to the other end of the country, to Southampton for a senior registrar post in medicine. After a long wait following the interview where 2 of us were discussed by the panel the other candidate was offered the job. Although I was disappointed, later on I was in fact thankful that this had been the outcome. The third post I applied for was a lecturer in medicine in the department of medicine at The Welsh National School of Medicine in Cardiff. Neither my wife nor I knew anything about Cardiff. Apart from 1 weekend trip to Tenby as a medical student I had never been to Wales and nor had Maureen. So, I flew down from Glasgow to meet Prof Robert Mahler the head of the dept. of Medicine. The medical school was relatively new and the University teaching hospital (University Hospital of Wales – UHW) had only been open for a year or so with a lot of clinical activity continuing at Cardiff Royal Infirmary. I was appointed lecturer in Medicine with special responsibility for teaching dental students some medicine to commence in August 1972. We also travelled to Cardiff to view the available housing stock. At that time there was a shortage of houses for sale in our price bracket but eventually bought a suitable property.

Back in Glasgow Prof Wilson ensured I had 1 month free of clinical duties to complete my MD thesis. We were excited to be going to new pastures but sad at leaving our families in Glasgow, particularly as we knew virtually no-one in Cardiff. When we left Glasgow, I felt that my training had been excellent. I had plenty of clinical experience in general medicine, endocrinology and thyroid disease in particular. I also had substantial teaching duties in Glasgow which afforded insight into methodology of clinical as well as lecturing aspects. In addition, I acquired the ability to undertake research projects and to understand how to write research papers. The opportunity to attend national and international meetings and present papers at many of these was also a very valued experience. As was pointed out to me many years later the department of medicine in Glasgow had provided appropriate resources and the stimulating atmosphere for research in all its forms.

For this much credit has to be given to Professor Sir Edward Wayne and his successor Professor Graham Wilson. Sir Edward, a Leeds graduate in chemistry prior to studying medicine had worked with Sir Thomas Lewis in London before WW2 and proceeded to the chair of Pharmacology at University of Sheffield before arriving in Glasgow as The Regius Professor of Medicine. He had a good sense of humour and could relate well with patients and staff alike. He had a disconcerting habit when on a ward round with staff and students surrounding him and behind him of suddenly stepping backwards. This caused much mirth in the students when he collided with some unfortunates who were ignorant of this practice. I am sure his chemical background led to his interest in establishing research and clinical aspects of iodine metabolism which brought much kudos to the department nationally and internationally. He was knighted for his contribution to the setting of a legal blood alcohol concentration in relation to vehicle driving in the UK. Graham Wilson, an Edinburgh medical graduate, came to Glasgow along a similar route to Wayne. He also worked in St Mary's hospital medical school and succeeded Wayne in Sheffield before arriving in Glasgow. He was more taciturn than Wayne but was clearly a national and international medical figure. His wife, Elizabeth, was a jolly woman, a family planning doctor who became head of family planning in Scotland. The couple had 6 children, partly, according to Graham, because they were the first to try out new contraceptive methods that did not work!

CHAPTER 10

Cardiff-Welsh National School of Medicine

And so to Cardiff. Married 2 and a half years with 2 small children, the youngest 10 weeks and knowing virtually no-one in Cardiff. Since obtaining the post I had been down to look at houses but there were hardly any on the market that were suitable. Maureen came with me once with our youngest child then aged about 1 month. We needed to hang the milk bottles out of the car window to cool them off before feeding. We settled on a semidetached 4-bedroom house in Penylan, not too far from the new hospital. This was being vacated by a doctor and his family who were moving to Burton-on-Trent to a consultant physician post and he charged me an extra £500 (about £8200 today) for the house as he knew my predicament. It turned out to be a good area and Maureen made new friends also with young children.

We were rather underwhelmed by the city of Cardiff in the early 1970s. The centre had been due for redevelopment, but this had been delayed due to lack of funding. The city was (and still is) a small city compared to Glasgow. However, it is a capital city but in the early 70s looked rather the worse for wear. The medical school was small compared to the one in Glasgow and it seemed to me that clinical teaching was not given the emphasis and organisation that I had been used to.

However, the new hospital was an impressive 900 bedded facility not 100% completed but operational. Some medical specialities, for example nephrology, remained in Cardiff Royal Infirmary. This was the traditional inner-city hospital and served as the casualty centre as well. I was working on the 7th (top) floor of the new hospital for 2 consultants, Prof Robert Mahler and Dr William Phillips. Robert Mahler had been appointed head of the department of Medicine some years before. Previously he was Prof of Metabolic medicine in Cardiff and was considered by his colleagues not to be very interested in clinical medicine. He had arrived in UK on the kinder transport in the late 1930s and had graduated in medicine from Edinburgh with a distinguished academic record. He had then worked in many centres in UK and USA on various aspects of diabetes and the rare disorders of glycogen storage disease. Dr William Phillips was born in Cardiff, son of a Professor of Education he had worked for Sir Thomas Lewis the famous cardiologist in London and was an astute general physician. He knew my previous boss in Glasgow Sir Edward Wayne and very much appreciated that I had a special interest in thyroid disease. I worked as a Lecturer in Medicine (senior registrar) for both these consultants for around a year before working for Dr Picton Thomas, an endocrinologist from West Wales. He was an excellent general physician and had also worked at The National Institutes of Health (NIH) in Bethesda, Maryland and knew a lot about renal physiology and steroids. He was, however, an abrasive character who sometimes was his own worst enemy.

By this time, I realised that my experience in Glasgow had equipped me well as a clinician, a medical teacher, and a researcher. However, the majority of my generation who aspired to academic medicine were really required to gain outside experience by working abroad for a period. I spent around a year exploring different avenues to achieve this without much success.

Once I had established the clinical setup and teaching arrangements in Cardiff, I could turn my attention to the MD. Although I did not manage to finish the thesis, in the months before leaving Glasgow, I did manage to complete the first (review) chapter and had several other chapters typed up in Glasgow. Late in 1972 or early 1973, not long after arriving in Cardiff, I sent the thesis off to Cambridge having received permission to proceed to MD. A year went by and I had not heard anything. Eventually, I wrote to Cambridge and discovered that they had sent the thesis back to the department in Glasgow! Unfortunately, no one in Glasgow had arranged for it to be sent to me in Cardiff! The message was that it was unsatisfactory and not fit in its current state to be examined by the viva voce exam, but no further data acquisition was required. I made the corrections rapidly and attended Cambridge for the viva. This was a terrifying experience as there were about 10 people sitting behind the long table but fortunately, I was only examined by 2 or 3 people led by the eminent physiologist Dr. Ian Glynn who subsequently became head of that department (and who died in July 2022). I was subsequently informed that I had passed. I was delighted by this and it justified the hard work I had put in in Glasgow, some of which was at nights and weekends.

I was now a lecturer with senior registrar status. This opened up a new area of responsibility namely not only making consultant like decisions on patients, but supervising activities and development of junior staff attached to the firm. I worked for Dr William Phillips, the senior physician in Wales who seemed to know most medical people in Wales as well as many in the Royal College in London. His ward rounds were interminably long but he was a shrewd physician if somewhat old fashioned in some of his therapeutic approaches. He was very kind to me and backed me up when there was controversy concerning clinical arrangements. Meanwhile I was participating fully in the clinical and social activities of the department and getting to know a bit about Wales. This was all very enjoyable, but I gradually realised that we had to get out of Cardiff at least for a while to broaden my research perspective. Most colleagues were achieving this by a posting in USA (the so called BTA-been to America experience) and I set about this task. It just so happened that there was an international thyroid conference in Glasgow in mid-1974. It was ironic that there had been no international thyroid meeting in Glasgow for all of the 6 years I had been attached to the department of Medicine. From my arrival in Cardiff, I had been working with my colleague Robert Elkeles, another lecturer in the department on a finding discovered by colleagues in the department of medical biochemistry. This involved the fact that high thyroid hormone concentrations in the blood could influence the release of an important hormone messenger (cyclic AMP) from the liver in animals. At that time there was a lot of interest in the assessment of thyroid status in the body not just by performing thyroid hormone blood tests and we were doing experiments in humans using this feature and correlating it with thyroid hormone levels in the blood.

So, in 1974 I drove up to Glasgow to attend the thyroid conference. I met thyroidologists from Europe as well as from USA and I contributed to the discussion in the meeting. The conference was about the mechanism of the action of thyroid hormone at the cell and whole body level and in Cardiff we had just published a paper on this in humans. This was led by my friend Robert Elkeles together with 2 distinguished biochemists.

Several international thyroid experts including some from USA and some from The Netherlands were there. Although I was not presenting a specific paper I stood up after one presentation and mentioned our results. The next day one of the clinical investigators, Dr Ken Sterling, from New York introduced himself to me and indicated that there might be a place in his lab for a research fellow. He was working at Columbia University based at the Veterans Administration hospital in the Bronx. He approached me and subsequently offered a place in his laboratory for 2 years. After making a few inquiries I accepted the post and this was due to start on July 1, 1975. My lecturer's post in Cardiff would be held open for me by appointing a locum.

I returned to Cardiff to discuss with Maureen, and we decided that if I could obtain funding this would be a great experience. I applied to the Medical Research Council but was unsuccessful. I did obtain some funding for travel from the Fulbright commission to add to a travel award from a Scottish charity and was a Fulbright Scholar. Meanwhile Sterling had indicated that he could fund my stay for up to 2 years through a grant from National Institutes of Health in Washington DC. Serendipitously this turned out to be very good because during the period we were in USA the £ fell from around $2.40 to $1.60 but as this grant was paid in dollars there were no ill effects. In Cardiff we had a visit from Prof Sheila Sherlock. She was a world authority on liver disease and after her lecture I was introduced to her and said that I was going to work for Sterling. She said 'Well you will have an exciting time!' We arranged to let our house, sell the car and made preparations to leave. A locum had been appointed to fill in for my job while I was away from Cardiff. Our two girls were growing up (4 and 3) and attending school in Cardiff. Maureen was not working at this time as there was certainly plenty to do looking after the children.

CHAPTER 11

New York- Columbia University

In preparation for going to New York I went ahead in June 1975 firstly to The International Thyroid Conference in Boston, an event that occurs every 5 years, leaving the family to come on later. I stayed with our friends John and Sarah Corson who had moved to USA permanently from Cardiff. I gave a paper on our work in Cardiff and met many workers in the field. The meeting was very successful academically as well as socially. I arrived in New York in mid-June and stayed with my father's 1st cousin Sydney Lazarus who was a pathologist living in Queens and working in a hospital in Brooklyn. He and Esther (his wife) were extremely kind to me and helped me orient myself to New York City. Sydney was Muriel's brother (had met me on my first trip to USA in 1960).

At this point I made contact with Sterling mainly to ask about accommodation near or close to the Bronx Veterans Administration Hospital where the lab was situated. He said, 'come for lunch.' I found that he lived near the hospital in probably the only respectable residential area of the Bronx. Lunch turned out to be 1 (yes 1) peanut and a coca cola. I had a feeling Sherlock was correct (not about lunch but the prospect of an exciting time). Sterling gave me a brief tour of the only safe residential section of the Bronx (Riverdale). He then took me in his car to some apartment blocks. I have to say that his behaviour towards some groups of girls sitting outside was not appropriate and I thought what is this guy really like?! I eventually found a 2-bedroom apartment in Riverdale, the only nice area of the Bronx overlooking the Hudson River and signed the rental agreement. It was unfurnished so I set about acquiring some items. There was a playground nearby and an open-air swimming pool within the apartment complex. I had already purchased a second-hand Ford automobile in Queens so I was able to take items of furniture to the apartment.

I transported a double mattress on the roof of my car. There was a basement in the hospital with furniture surplus to requirements and this was very useful. The family duly flew into Kennedy airport and I was delighted to see them. Esther was very kind and brought a cooked chicken over from her apartment in Queens. Our immediate neighbours in the apartment block were doctors and teachers and they were all very kind and helpful; one couple who had 2 children with a husband who was a teacher. Another 2 couples where both husbands were doctors.

I started in the lab, which was small, with a staff of a post doc (Hungarian who sadly died in 2018), a senior technician and Sterling. It was a great privilege to immerse myself in particular aspects of thyroid hormone action without clinical, teaching or administrative duties. We all worked from 9am to 6pm and met at 5 pm or so to discuss the day's experimental results and plan the experimental regime for the next day. Our lab in the VA was part of Columbia University which had some world famous people attending and was about 10 minutes from where we lived. Although it had a security check to get into the car park it was not without incident. There was a mugging in the elevator and there was a methadone programme for ex US forces who had served in Vietnam. Fortunately, the lab was relatively isolated and there were no problems. I soon realised that several world class labs were in the hospital doing research. The most famous was that of Rosalyn Yalow the Nobel prize winner inventor of radioimmunoassay (used first for measurement of hormones such as Insulin and thyroid hormones in the blood). She had achieved this in cooperation with Solomon Berson but as the latter had passed away it could not be awarded to him.

The research post in Dr Sterling's lab at the Veteran's Administration hospital in the Bronx was stimulating. We were investigating thyroid hormone action on the energy organelles in the cell namely mitochondria. This was controversial as most workers were fixated on the nucleus of the cell as a target for thyroid hormone. Several labs tried to replicate our results but could not do so. Even when a physiologist working in another lab came over to our lab to observe our experiments (all in rats) he could not repeat these in the other lab. We were involved in confirming and characterising the nature of the attachment (binding) of thyroid hormone to mitochondria of thyroid responsive cells. We used liver cells from rats so I spent many months killing rats and extracting the mitochondria from liver cells.

Around the second weekend in the apartment was July 4th and we travelled to Washington to stay with Ronnie and Pam Barr. He was working in The National Institutes of Health (NIH) in haematology and was one of my flat mates in Glasgow, while his wife Pam had been at school with Maureen. She had trained as a physiotherapist and had shared a flat in Glasgow with Maureen. Unfortunately, our car broke down about halfway and Ronnie very kindly came to fetch us. We had a great weekend, one of the highlights being our first hearing of Billy Connolly! Returning to New York I was informed of the tragic death of Muriel's son Robert. I was not able to attend the funeral but went to see Muriel and his father, Mortimer Sackler soon afterwards.

In the fall when school started the girls went to a local primary on a yellow school bus which picked them up from our apartment block and brought them back in the afternoon which was very convenient. Meanwhile Maureen decorated our apartment and started to make friends. We all had a good time in New York seeing family as well as liaising with Suzanne, my sister, who had started her PhD in Harvard, Mass. Columbia University College of Physicians and Surgeons was in upper Manhattan so I would drive down there to the endocrine journal club and sometimes attend the thyroid clinic. This left Maureen on her own but she eventually started a design course by correspondence. There was also a small playground near the apartment building and in the summer of 1976, we joined the swimming pool in the apartment complex. This was a success as we had made many friends by this time. In the winter of 75/76 skiing was the holiday of choice in Vermont with the Corsons staying in a superb A framed house.

In the lab I found Sterling to be highly intelligent but he owned and operated a bad temper. He also swore a lot; indeed, I learnt many new words and phrases. He knew everyone of importance in the thyroid field and received many papers requesting review. He often gave them to me to see what I made of them before delivering his verdict. He would come into the lab in the morning and say (re a particular paper he had been asked to review) 'I think we will wee wee all over this one'! One problem we had was that the results we obtained with mitochondria were still not being confirmed by other labs and also that most of the work on thyroid hormone action in USA was concentrated on the interaction of the hormone with the cell nucleus. Nevertheless, we stuck to our guns and although techniques have changed markedly there is still interest in the findings.

In the summer of '76 we flew to Denver to stay with Burt Golub and his wife Lee. I had met Burt in 1960 in

Boston before he graduated and he was now a physician in infectious disease in Denver. We rented a car to drive to San Francisco to a meeting and then did a circular tour via Los Angeles, visiting relatives there and going on to Las Vegas, New Mexico and back to Denver to fly back to New York. A highlight of course was visiting the Grand Canyon and overall we all had a great trip. We all went to Disneyland at Anaheim in California; I think Maureen and I had a more enjoyable time than the children! On return we found out that Maureen was pregnant and therefore decided to return to Cardiff at end of September. We really could not afford obstetric delivery costs in USA. We also thought that, if it was a boy, it would be better to be a British prime minister that an American president! Today I would not wish to hold either office.

Other trips included visiting Tufts Hospital, Boston to give a lecture as well as visiting with my sister Suzanne who was living in Cambridge Mass. having started her PhD at Harvard University. We also travelled to Boston and Atlantic City for meetings. The American Thyroid Association met in Toronto in 1976 and it was exciting to attend and have lunch in the revolving CN tower. Later, I was lucky enough to be given a chance to attend The Laurentian Hormone meeting held in September. This meeting consisted of 1 hour long papers given at the start and end of the day with ample time for discussion. Lectures were given by endocrine experts in the field. The middle of the day was your own for walking, golf and other recreation and networking in the beautiful landscape of the Laurentian mountains north of Montreal. On returning to New York there was about 1 week to go before we departed for Wales. Our sojourn in USA had been full of new experiences in addition to dedicated lab work; meeting relatives, travel, seeing diverse cultures and more but it was time to return home.

From a professional point of view, I had learnt a huge amount about lab work. I was a co-author on 4 publications including 2 in Science (a world-famous journal) and 1 in Annual review of Physiology. I had also been elected a member of The American Thyroid Association. I would also like to record my heartfelt thanks to Peter Milch PhD the Hungarian who had walked from Budapest to freedom with his mother in 1956. He was dependable but left the lab not long after I arrived home and went into the pharmaceutical industry. My thanks too go to Milton Brenner who had been the technician with Sterling for many years and knew his foibles and moods. I thank Dr Sterling for employing me. Actually, we got on most of the time. After I left, Sterling phoned Milton one day, but he was not there. Sterling always came in at around 9.30 and expected everyone to be working. He arrived not best pleased and said to Milton where the ---- were you. Milton replied 'We were all round at Yalow's. 'And what the ---- were you doing there? Well, she had just learnt that she had won the Nobel prize Dr Sterling'!

When I left for UK Sterling still had part of the NIH grant and he persuaded a delightful Japanese doctor who had been working in Boston to come to the lab. This was a boon for us as he took over our apartment which was fine for his family as it had been for ours. We were sorry to return home at this juncture, but I thought not much more could be achieved on the research front and the baby was due in 3 months. We flew back to Wales and arrived in Cardiff on Oct 1$^{st.}$ It all seemed very small in Cardiff compared to New York. The whole US experience both scientific and social was very rewarding and we were sorry to leave.

We returned to our house which we had rented out to dentists and started to pick up life in Wales. It was pouring with rain and rained solidly for 6 weeks which made up for the record drought that had occurred in UK during that summer. Indeed, Cardiff had appeared in the New York Times reporting on the settlement of many houses in the area due to the drought. The girls returned to the same primary school but their Americanisation was noted. Our younger one, Jenny, had an argument with one of her classmates and was heard to say in a strong Bronx accent 'Do you wanna fat lip?! Maureen was nearly 7 months pregnant when we arrived home and had carried the pregnancy in NYC with almost no antenatal care. We were blessed with a healthy baby boy (Simon) in the middle of December and all the family were delighted! Maureen was able to spend a few days in hospital and was very well when she arrived home.

We had also arrived back in UK in time for me to attend a dinner in Glasgow to mark the retirement of my father. This was a pleasurable evening when glowing tributes were paid to Dad.

CHAPTER 12

The Doldrums

I resumed work as a lecturer in Cardiff but was now looking around for either a senior lecturer post or a consultant physician post. Eventually a senior lecturer post was advertised based in the main teaching hospital in Cardiff. Unfortunately, I was not successful, and the post went to an outsider who was working in Manchester. Moreover, in anticipation of a position in Cardiff I had obtained a mortgage to purchase a house. This had been exceedingly difficult and there we were on a bank holiday with a mortgage but having to decline the purchase! I was devastated and embarrassed by this as colleagues had expected me to obtain the post. In retrospect I had not prepared properly for the interview and had not been given any advice or practice. It was kind of Robert Mahler to write to my father explaining the situation. Reflecting on the time since returning from New York I would say that I was probably a bit too self-assured but I received no help from anyone on the type of interview that I might have for the first post which I did not obtain.

Having failed in Cardiff I thought it reasonable to apply for a National Health Service post that was advertised in Shrewsbury/Telford. I did visit the site but was not placed on the short list. Meanwhile in Cardiff I was made a locum consultant/senior lecturer with clinical work in the main hospital. There was a lot of movement in the consultant staff at that time and as a result a senior lectureship in Medicine was advertised in Llandough hospital. This was the hospital on the west side of Cardiff and afforded more independence than a post in University Hospital. There was a very collegiate group of consultants there who were always ready to help and I was successful with my application and started there in April 1978, moving house in July of that year. We had managed to purchase a 4-bedroom detached villa in Cyncoed, Cardiff which suited all the family and we have been very pleased with it during that last 45 years or so. I kept my office in UHW together with attendance at a medical and thyroid clinic. I also did a general medicine clinic in Barry, a few miles west of Llandough so I was covering the whole city of Cardiff and surrounding areas. However, doing a clinic in Barry every week proved too much so I cut this back to once every 2 weeks. Our firm also had 2 different groups of medical students to teach and this was hard work for myself and my registrar. Fortunately, I had inherited a team of doctors from the previous consultant including a registrar who was on a 2 year appointment. This provided valuable continuity for his/her training and involvement in research. This would be impossible today as there are no teams attached to one consultant. This is one of the factors contributing to low morale in hospital staff.

Having settled in Cardiff I started attending endocrine and thyroid meetings some of which were in London. This gave me the chance to see Michele, my youngest sister, as she had moved there after her undergraduate career in Edinburgh University. She had studied economics and other cognate subjects and after graduation attained an MSc in London.

I looked after a lot of general medical patients which I liked and I was assisted by a registrar who was with me for 2 years, a houseman, senior house officer and a senior registrar for most of the time. Although I had no research fellow, I involved the registrar in thyroid and other projects. The senior registrars were mostly training in chest disease and came to me for experience in general medicine. We did a lot of teaching of medical students mostly round the bedside which I really enjoyed. There were 4 of us general physicians who got on very well and ran a coronary care unit and well as the overdose unit for Cardiff.

Academically however, I was somewhat in the doldrums as I was not part of a thyroid research group and had difficulty raising money. I hit on the idea of doing some hypertension research for pharmaceutical companies. This proved variably successful but did help to pay for some thyroid work and I was able to employ a part time research nurse. I soon discovered that being a consultant could be a lonely job in that the buck stops here. I was on call for emergencies 1 day in 4 and 1 weekend in 4 but I was shielded to some extent by my team. In the absence of mobile phones, I really could not leave the house and I did have to go into the hospital in the middle of the night but this was not frequent. On the plus side I found myself covering the whole city of Cardiff, along with colleagues for general medicine and doing the thyroid clinic in UHW with a surgeon.

JS Hilary (Larry) Wade was a very experienced general surgeon who had been awarded an MC during the Second World War when operating in the North African Desert. He was also an excellent thyroid surgeon and, for a while, the keeper of wines at the Royal College of Surgeons in London. Having a registrar post of 2 years duration allowed me to develop some clinically based research which I did and published. I also became involved in various aspects of medical school life and started to attend endocrine, thyroid and some hypertension meetings in UK and abroad. At about this time Robert Mahler announced that he was taking a sabbatical for a year to work on lipid metabolism in Sweden. Not long after he returned to Cardiff, he announced that he was resigning his chair of medicine and moving to Northwick Park Hospital in London. My colleague Robert Elkeles was there at the time. Mahler also undertook the editorship of the Journal of the Royal College of Physicians which I think he greatly enjoyed. So, what about the succession in Cardiff?

CHAPTER 13

Arrival of Reg

Following intense speculation, the field for the chair of medicine narrowed down to 2 candidates: Prof William (Bill) Ascher, Professor of Nephrology at Cardiff Royal Infirmary and Prof Reginald (Reg) Hall, Professor of Endocrinology at Newcastle University Medical School. They were both excellent academics and clinicians. Bill Asscher was the local favourite but several of us in Cardiff knew that Reg Hall was a very strong candidate. I had met him when I was in Glasgow, and he was clearly a leader in the thyroid field in UK and beyond. He was very thorough and supported everyone according to their capabilities. Before the interviews in Cardiff, he spent 2 hours with me on the telephone to understand the medical curriculum in The Welsh National School of Medicine. When Prof (now Sir) Dillwyn Williams and I attended the European Thyroid Association in Newcastle in summer 1979 all the British people just assumed Reg was going to be appointed. Although we hoped that would be the case, we knew Bill had much justified support. In the event Reg was appointed and started in 1980. We were all delighted and looked forward to putting Cardiff on the national and international map in endocrinology and thyroidology.

The early 80s are now a bit of a blur. I was a busy clinician both in general medicine and in thyroid disease. My 'firm' at LLandough was also busy with teaching commitments to 2 different years of clinical students and I was serving on various academic and NHS committees. I had become a fellow of the Royal College of Physicians and Surgeons of Glasgow in 1979 and in 1983 was elected a fellow of The Royal College of Physicians of London. It became clear that much of thyroid disease was driven by abnormal immunological responses and I attended a course at The Middlesex hospital in London on immunology to further my understanding of the subject. My colleagues, Bernard Rees Smith, Alan McGregor and Tony Weetman, all of whom Reg had brought from Newcastle, knew a lot of immunology and were very active in research. During the decade I was involved in papers on thyroid disease as well as hypertension, iodine, beta blocking drugs and medical education.

In 1979 one of my father's colleagues from Glasgow who was Prof of Pharmacology in Cardiff proposed me as a fellow of the Royal College of Physicians and Surgeons of Glasgow. This proposal was accepted, and I became FRCP(Glas). I was establishing my clinical credentials especially as the 'go to' person for thyroid disease. Prof Reg Hall had arrived in 1980 and during the next decade I participated in many papers including studies on Lithium, beta blockers, thyroid antibodies, blood pressure management, case reports and Graves' disease as well as Iodine. Reg was a huge stimulating influence on everyone he came into contact with and the department flourished. Alan McGregor and Tony Weetman were very helpful to me, both going on to distinguished careers in England. I had also appointed a research fellow, Dr. (now Prof.) Marian Ludgate, who obtained her PhD in Cardiff. She was supported with moneys obtained from a pharmaceutical company. She fitted in perfectly to the thyroid scene and over the years worked with McGregor and Weetman on immunological developments in thyroid disease. She also worked with a very distinguished group of scientists in Brussels. She and I were associated with around 14 papers or so during the ensuing years.

I had been the Welsh national representative on ICCIDD (International Council for Control of Iodine Deficiency Disorders) for a number of years but this involved nothing in particular. My interest in iodine was rekindled by David Phillips who came as my registrar and then by being asked to contribute along with others to reviewing national developments at the annual iodine meeting just before the ETA took place.

I then went to Senegal to conduct the study of goitre and iodised oil treatment.

In the early 1980s Reg Hall was asked to give a lecture on thyroid disease in pregnancy particularly the postpartum period. He realised that he did not know much about this area of thyroidology and set about conducting a survey with McGregor and other colleagues resulting in a paper in the British Medical Journal showing that thyroid disease in the postpartum was indeed quite common. I became involved later in the decade after Reg had retired due to his cardiac transplant and Alan McGregor had moved to Kings College Hospital in London as Professor of Medicine. Over the next 2 decades this line of enquiry resulted in over 50 publications not including several book chapters and contributions to meetings. It was due to these contributions that I became a Fellow of The Royal College of Obstetricians and Gynaecologists FRCOG (ad eundem) in 2005. By this time, we were well on the way to completing the antenatal screening for thyroid function in early pregnancy and performing the controlled trial of thyroid hormone in pregnancy.

CHAPTER 14

Abu Dabi

About 4 years after Reg started in Cardiff he was diagnosed as having cardiac amyloid. This was, and still is, a rare but devastating condition. At that time there was no specific therapy for the disease but one option was cardiac transplantation. Reg immediately signed up for this and had the procedure carried out in Harefield hospital in 1984. He survived and went on to live for another 10 years with the amazing help of his wife Molly, a consultant Rheumatologist.

In 1989 I was at home one Sunday morning relaxing. A colleague (Professor of Dermatology) rang and asked whether I could see a Sheik? I said yes but when and he replied as soon as possible. He then told me that the address was in Abu Dhabi, and I would be picked up from the airport! By the afternoon I was speeding along to Heathrow airport to catch a flight to Abu Dhabi and was duly met by a very large Mercedes. I had left my car in the short stay car park in Heathrow.

I arrived in the Sheik's private hospital where I was to see him. The whole family had been having X rays during the day ending with His Excellency. I had to wait for his arrival and was slightly nervous being Jewish in an Arab county. He did eventually arrive in the examination room, and I started to take a medical history However, it soon became apparent that he did not wish to talk about this; he merely wanted me to examine him. I was examining the back of his chest when the British nurse who was assisting said are you Dr Lazarus? Yes, I said. Any relation of Sam Lazarus? I looked at her amazed and slightly nonplussed. He is my father. She had been working in Glasgow in the private sector in the nursing home assisting my father!

Meanwhile, I detected some abnormalities on clinical examination of the chest in the base of one of the lungs. I then reviewed the X-Rays. Actually, they were of poor quality, but it was just possible to make out some changes approximating to the site of my findings. It turned out that His Excellency had been in Switzerland to have his annual medical check-up. This was reported as normal, so he proceeded to Morocco where he spent a few days with the King. However, on return to Abu Dhabi he developed a cough and mild breathlessness and was found to have an elevated temperature, hence the request for a consultant medical opinion. In discussion with his General Practitioner, an excellent Sudanese doctor from Khartoum, antibiotics were prescribed. I then retreated to the 1st class hotel where I had dinner and an excellent bottle of white wine. Alcohol consumption was permitted only in this hotel. The following day the GP came round to the hotel to say that his excellency felt better. I replied, 'Oh that's good. Perhaps I can fly home later'. No came the response. You need to stay until his temperature comes down to normal! I must have grimaced because that could take a long time. Anyway, I had to stay and I made use of the big Mercedes and driver and went to see the petroleum museum and watched the camel racing in my room at the hotel. I was not best pleased but fortunately, after a further 48 hrs I received the good news that his temperature had indeed come down. The GP visited and asked what my fee was. I had no idea what to charge so settled on £160, quite a lot for 1989. He had no problem obtaining this amount and in addition he presented me with a wristwatch which had diamonds round the circumference and at every hour on the clock face. It is an American genre similar to a Rolex but not so big and chunky. I have worn it for 35 years and it keeps good time. I did not see the patient again but managed to obtain a flight to Dubai to change planes for the flight to London. This was a first-class ticket and although it was near midnight, I enjoyed a superb dinner. When I returned to London, I found that my parking costs in London were in excess of my fee but I had to pay and drive back to Cardiff. Overall, an interesting experience treating the super wealthy. I later learnt that he had the same clinician come every year to check his prostate as this was the same finger. He lived for a long time and died some 20 years later.

CHAPTER 15

Senegal – A Goitre Study

Late in the 1980s my sister Suzanne, who had studied in Oxford and gained a PhD at Harvard in health evaluation, moved to Dakar in Senegal to set up a regional office to support the development of national diarrhoea control programmes in 6 West African countries. Senegal was known to have a problem with iodine deficiency and goitre, and I realised that her residence in the country provided an ideal base for field studies. I had never been to a developing country before and was excited to have this possibility. I went in late 1989 for a week and started making plans to evaluate goitre and thyroid function in 7 villages in the Casamance area of Senegal. Suzanne introduced me to the Regional Nutrition Institute for West Africa Dakar (ORANA). I obtained some financial support from the Royal Society in London as well as a grant from the European Union. The rest of our supplies were begged, borrowed or stolen. Flying back to Senegal was an adventure in itself. I was wearing a shirt with 2 pockets on the chest stuffed with needles for taking blood. My suitcase was packed with syringes and other paraphernalia which certainly would not have been allowed today. I also had bags of drug samples given to me by pharmaceutical representatives! I was lucky not to be accused of drug peddling!

When I returned in early 1990 a team from ORANA was assembled from there with 2 jeeps, 4 or 5 assistants and myself to travel to Velingara, the local township. This entailed a long journey on the North side of the river Gambie before turning south and reaching our destination. The Gambie River almost divides Senegal in two and is located in the middle of The Gambia. I wondered why a country is just a long ribbon of land? When the British were sailing along the river in the 19th century, they decided that any land within gunshot range of the boat was going to be a British colony. A great way of surveying. To this day the borders are the same and the country has some quintessentially British quirks like driving on the left and the availability of McVitie's digestive biscuits. English is the principal lingua franca.

At that time the Medical Research Council had a base in Banjul the capital and an outpost in Basse Sante Su, a dusty little village in the east of The Gambia. My colleague Dr (now Prof) Peter Smyth from Dublin agreed to perform ultrasound examinations of the thyroid and was able to rent a portable ultrasound machine which he transported from Dublin. The whole area was very poor with, for example no running water in any of the 7 villages we visited. Water was drawn from a nearby well with a plastic bucket and a string. In addition, there was no light available when darkness fell. A burning cob contained in a discarded aluminium container was the only illumination. Working with the local health authorities we arrived at the first village where a consultation was held with the village chief as to our intentions. A long queue of women materialised as if from nowhere and we started to take blood samples and to acquire a urine sample for iodine measurement. In return we gave them a dose of oral iodised oil in order to improve their thyroid function and, in some people, to reduce the size of their goitre. For those subjects who wished it I held a medical consultation service. On completion we returned to the hospital in Velingara and used their centrifuge to spin the blood to obtain the serum which was stored in a refrigerator. I learnt and appreciated the importance of the cold chain which we all take for granted in developed countries. We had a nurse with us who was very helpful but I noticed he was keeping all the needles we used for venepuncture. When questioned he said if he did not keep them there would be no method of vaccinating the population! It was certainly a different set of priorities. After 10 days I flew back to Dakar in a small plane with the samples and stored them in my sister's fridge until the return trip to UK. The pilot had to be extra careful as Concorde was preparing to land at Dakar just as we arrived.

The whole trip was an adventure and I arranged a follow up in 6 months and 1 year to check on thyroid volume by ultrasound and other details. I was most grateful to my sister in Dakar for helping to facilitate this project and for the use of her domestic fridge for storing samples until my return to Cardiff. An essential requirement was to obtain some dry ice to store the samples during return to UK. We scoured Dakar one night and eventually discovered some for sale in a very undesirable area of the city. It was also fascinating to meet her friends resident in Dakar as well as professionals (usually American) who were experts in their subjects and were passing through the city. Arriving home after the first trip to Southern Senegal my wife almost did not recognise me as I had lost so much weight! While in the field leading the group, I mostly ate packaged biscuits, coffee, oranges and occasionally a meal at the medical officer's house; this was to prevent any gastrointestinal problems and was successful.

The medical officer, who kindly found me a place to sleep near the laboratory, was a captain in the Senegalese army and was doing duty in this unpopular area of the country. He was the only doctor for approximately 100,000 people and treatments for various conditions were primitive. His operating theatre certainly did not look clean and was adorned with a page from a standard surgical textbook for methodology of hernia operation. Many small children had an enlarged spleen due to chronic malaria, the only treatment being a dose of Chloroquine every so often. The latter was kept in a grimy bottle on a dirty windowsill. Several decades later it is exciting to think that a vaccine against Malaria is very close to being available with the prospect of preventing the disease and saving countless lives. One night I was at his house for dinner and he asked how the project was progressing. I replied that generally things were ok but just that day we had visited a village and not succeeded in obtaining any blood samples because the village elders had said no. Come with me he said and bring your implements. At 8 pm we drove to the village in his jeep and after he had had a few words with the village chiefs we started taking blood and urine samples. The only light was from burning corn on the cob husks in the aluminium tray as described above. I must admit to not questioning him as to what he said but his orders seemed pretty firm. So, we toiled into the night, returned with the samples and then had to spend more time processing them for cool storage.

When I returned 6 months later it was the height of summer and very hot indeed. The captain invited me into his office which was mercifully air conditioned. After some desultory questions and discussion, he opened a filing draw... and extracted a bottle of Scotch whisky! Sometime later I staggered out into the heat to go to sleep, a memorable evening. The result of these 3 visits were published in 1992 and, in brief, showed that goitre prevalence in 7 villages in 502 people was 62%. The response to 480mg oral iodised oil showed a significant reduction in goitre prevalence after one year. That goitre was at least in part due to iodine deficiency was confirmed by measurement of iodine in the urine in a smaller number of residents receiving iodine to those that did not. However, there was a significant variation in the goitre size in the population of this area suggesting that iodine deficiency was not the only cause. I could not manage to satisfactorily evaluate other factors such as diet or genetics. We did attempt to perform some detailed dietary surveys which was an interesting exercise. The field workers demanded an increase in their wages, and I remember this resulting in negotiation under a very large Mango tree with their discussions being translated into French and eventually to English!

The whole experience in Senegal had introduced me to aspects of public health in the field. I became familiar with another area of thyroidology. While leading the group I found that I had to be alert from the moment I woke up until lights out. We managed to do a lot on a minimum budget and the entire process increased my awareness of how difficult studies in the field can be. Earlier studies of goitre in S America, Switzerland and remote areas of Indonesia emphasise these difficulties. I was most grateful to Suzanne for facilitating the whole visit. As a result of this our daughters Tracey and Jenny came out to develop a project relating to an elective study being conducted by Jenny. Tracey spoke good French and was able to assist her. Michele, my youngest sister, appeared on a tourist visit. Later on, she met Neil Davidson, now her partner. She gave birth to Cal who is now 25 and works in finance in London. She now practices hypnotherapy and lives in Stroud.

CHAPTER 16

Thyroid and other Sudies

Post partum Thyroid Disease

Back in Cardiff clinical work proceeded as normal and was very busy. Our studies on postpartum thyroiditis were also going ahead and we became interested in the Clinical and Immunological aspects of the condition as well as psychiatric and radiological aspects in addition to epidemiological and advisory inputs on future pregnancies. I was chair of this group and we eventually were studying probably the largest group in the UK producing many papers and other published material. [see p. 84 et seq]

Iodine Metabolism in Sri Lanka

In the middle of the 90s my colleague Dr (now Prof) Kuvera Premawardhana, a consultant physician and endocrinologist, asked me whether I could help him assess the iodine status in his country of birth, Sri Lanka. I jumped at this opportunity to work in his homeland which was not an underdeveloped nation like Senegal. We set about developing a plan and raising some finance. Kuvera had a contact in Sri Lanka who had access to The World Bank, and we obtained funding for activities in the country from that institution. We arrived in Colombo Airport at 5 am and were met by a delegation from the world bank and also Kuvera's parents. There was a well-known area of goitre in women described some years before we arrived but when we were travelling through the area, I said to Kuvera 'These young women seem absolutely normal!' Subsequently we visited them at a well-known garment manufacturing factory and confirmed this observation. Then a driver with a van was procured for us and our aim was to examine 15-year-old schoolgirls in different parts of the country and to obtain appropriate samples. We selected a sample of schools and arranged to be present at the morning assembly to select the girls. We had obtained appropriate permission and ethical approval, and the schools were very pleased to see us. We selected those in the right age group, obtained the blood sample and a thyroid ultrasound was performed. We also assessed their nutritional status by measuring their arm circumference and weighing them. Then we moved on to the next school in a different part of the country. We could not visit the Northern part of the island because of security concerns. On the second visit my whole family came over and we had a delightful holiday on a small island in the south. Later, I received an invitation to speak at the Sri Lankan Endocrine Society and also after that at the Sri Lankan Society of Internal Medicine where I was the chief guest. The introduction to this meeting was a dance routine by invited dancers as well as very loud instrumentation.

We were thrilled to tour the Buddhist monuments as well as viewing the elephants, large and small, in a river location. We also visited a tea estate and learnt something of the problems of the workers at these institutions. Overall, I visited the country several times and our work resulted in several papers over about a decade. There are many people to thank, both medical and non-medical, without whose help we could not have accomplished this work. It is now tragic to note the sharp economic decline in this beautiful country and I fear it will take many years to return to previous prosperity.

Ghana

In 1994 I noticed an advert to perform a landscape analysis of medical care and facilities in Ghana together with a hospital administrator from the West Indies. I applied and after an interview in Sheffield I was appointed to the post. The project was funded by The Overseas Development Association (ODA) and my sister was a friend of one of the advisors to ODA. Whether this was connected with my appointment I do not know. McNaught and I arrived in Ghana and travelled up country to start the survey. We were not required to document services in the capital, Accra, but to concentrate on hospitals (mostly built by the British) in as many areas as possible. I found the experience of interviewing the hospital management quite stimulating as we were able to pinpoint problems from the outside. We were well received and eventually collaborated to produce a report (McNaught A, Lazarus JH. Report: Hospital management consultancy for the Ministry of Health – Ghana. UNECIA, May pp43, 1994).

Our investigations into postpartum thyroid disease were resulting in many papers describing the various clinical aspects of the syndrome; our group also actively investigated the pathophysiology and immunology of PPT resulting in another flurry of published papers and presentations at different meetings. As leader of the group, I was elected as a Fellow of The Royal College of Obstetricians and Gynaecologists (FRCOG ad eundem) in 2005, recommended by Mr Peter Bowen-Simkins, a former treasurer of that college and the late Dr Matt Carty the then vice-president of the college and a medical student in my year in Glasgow. At the ceremony there were a number of distinguished obstetricians who were also receiving Fellowships ad eundem. After the ceremony all of us were ushered onto a boat in the Thames with our wives/partners and proceeded to the tower of London for a tour. This was followed by a dinner at the college which was attended by many young doctors who had become members. Altogether a memorable day.

In the early part of the 2000s my colleague Prof Maurice Scanlon had been in contact with a Romanian Professor of Endocrinology from Bucharest, Prof Mihai Coculescu. Coculescu was in charge of the Endocrine hospital in Bucharest but was unable to fulfil his academic potential because of the political situation. However, following the overthrow and execution of President Ceausescu he was allowed to travel abroad and quickly established academic contacts in Oxford, Bristol and Cardiff as well as in Denmark. There was funding from the EU to support these ventures and to encourage 2-way traffic. I went out to Bucharest primarily to teach medical students and found the experience very rewarding. The students were able and studied the different clinical branches of medicine in hospitals dedicated solely to the specialty eg Cardiology, Endocrinology etc. The 'wards' in the endocrine hospital were very small and the patients jammed very close together. This was because any patient with an endocrine condition in say the North of Romania had to come down to Bucharest for evaluation as the only blood tests or appropriate radiological facilities at that time were in the capital. The countryside was desperately poor with transportation relying on horse drawn carts. However, in Bucharest there were still many fine old buildings built before WW2 including a concert hall where I was privileged to hear an excellent concert. My first view of the Ceausescu's palace was jaw dropping. The building was grotesquely large with massive walls and staircases. Along the avenue leading to this monstrosity are large houses given to the favourites of the dictator. I have returned to

Romania several times making visits to Iasi in the northeast, Timisoara in the West and other conurbations to take part in meetings. The local medical communities were always very cordial and grateful for the attendance of many members of the western European medical community.

By this time Coculescu had become a Fellow of The American College of Endocrinology, an organisation of which I was also a fellow. In 2003 I received the distinguished clinician award from the ACE. The society paid for me and my wife to travel to San Diego to receive this and I am grateful to Coculescu for his recommendation. It was a signal honour for me. The last time I was in Romania there was a meeting in Craiova and Prof Coculescu was there; little did I know that he was suffering from a terminal blood disorder and sadly died some months later. He had provided the energy and spark in endocrinology after the fall of Ceausescu and deserves huge credit for that. Today Romania is still the second largest country in the old iron curtain group after Poland with a population of around 20 million. It was elected to the European Union and has benefitted hugely from this but unfortunately there is still too much corruption in public life which is retarding progress.

Around the turn of the 20th century I was reading the New England Journal of Medicine one late afternoon. There was an interesting article which caught my eye on maternal thyroid deficiency during pregnancy and subsequent neuropsychological development of the child by Jim Haddow and colleagues from USA. Their group showed that in 7–9-year-old children, high levels of maternal thyrotropin (TSH, the pituitary hormone that controls thyroid function) derived from stored serum samples taken during pregnancy, performance of a range of intelligence tests was inferior to children of mothers with normal levels of TSH taken at the same stage of pregnancy. These results suggested that screening for thyroid function in early pregnancy and appropriate treatment with thyroid hormone may be indicated. I thought this was exciting and contacted Professor Nicholas Wald at St Bartholomew's Hospital who was not an author but who had been thanked as an advisor. Following several visits to see him in London we decided to apply for funding to conduct a randomised trial where women were assigned to a screening or control group in early pregnancy. The women in the screening group were given thyroid hormone if their levels indicated hypothyroidism (underactivity). The control group had their levels measured after delivery although the blood samples were also taken in early pregnancy and stored until delivery. The grant application was successful (Wellcome Trust and Compagnia di San Paulo, Turin) and we performed the trial over several years as we studied more than 21,000 women. The study took a long time but the results were published in 2012 (in New England Journal of Medicine). In brief they showed that antenatal screening and maternal treatment for hypothyroidism did not result in improved cognitive function in children at 3 years of age. While this was disappointing the study was the first of its type and has opened the way for many studies on the role of thyroid hormone in neurodevelopment during the last decade. It also emphasised the importance of collaboration in medical research, and I am very grateful to Nick Wald and his colleagues for their input and collaboration.

CHAPTER 17

The Children

During the nineties all three children had started university, the eldest having had a gap year in Paris and Israel was about to go to Hull University to read European Studies (French and Spanish) and the second gaining a place in Oxford to read Geography. Maureen and I were enormously proud of them on these achievements. Our son, Simon was studying for A levels in Monmouth School prior to being accepted by University of Birmingham to study materials science.

All the children subsequently graduated from University and Maureen and I were very proud to attend the graduation ceremonies in Hull, Oxford and Birmingham. It is worth documenting their collective subsequent progress as they have all moved into different fields of activity.

Tracey spent a year in Brussels working initially for the estate agency Knight Frank and then for the Brussels office of Greater London Enterprise. She shared an apartment with a school friend and sometimes some others who were passing through. The first apartment they had was above an African bar however they later moved to a more salubrious part of town in a modern flat which was more comfortable and secure. She also found time to enrol for a master's degree in international politics at The Free University of Brussels and successfully completed the course and was awarded the degree of MA. She then returned to London and worked for Greater London Enterprise as a researcher and fund writer. She also gained a post graduate diploma in History of Art from the Courtauld Institute emphasising her interest in art and specialised in the work of Caravaggio. I think she should have gone on to complete an MA degree but she decided not to. She had met Vincenzo who hailed from Puglia in Italy when she was in Barcelona as part of her undergraduate studies as an Erasmus student from Hull. They married in 2000 and have 1 daughter, Sofia, who is our only grandchild.

For some years now she has been working at Leighton House Museum in Holland Park in Kensington.

Jenny did not pursue a 'gap year' and went straight to Jesus College Oxford to read Geography. She enjoyed meeting new friends at Oxford and found the course very comprehensive. In fact, it encompassed so many diverse areas of study that when she graduated it was not clear to her which career path to follow. Then she had a gap year which included grape picking in Italy, working in a ski resort and volunteering in Mexico in rural communities. After spending some time in London in various jobs she was awarded a Mountbatten internship programme in New York for a year. On return to UK, she followed in her father's footsteps and graduated in Medicine in Sheffield. She is now a General Practitioner and lives in Bath.

Simon graduated in materials science and technology at The University of Birmingham in 1998 and proceeded to Imperial College London to complete a Masters in Composite Materials in 2000. He also learnt how to work in a bar, a useful qualification. He then attended Cranfield University to study for a PhD and was awarded this in 2005 in Composite materials. Following a research officer post in Cranfield he then took 6 months off, travelling to S America. After this rewarding break, he started work in a company in Banbury which specialised in designing, qualifying, developing and manufacturing composite products for the aerospace industry. He remains there as an engineering manager.

CHAPTER 18

The Health Service

The health service and the medical school had a myriad of committees, probably far too many and some of them were acting only as talking shops. I did want to play my part in those committees I thought useful and as a consultant attended the now defunct division of medicine. I eventually did a spell as chairman but by that time it was losing its power in that its recommendations were not being listened to by other bodies higher up. This happened again when I chaired the HMSSC (hospital medical staff subcommittee) and taught me that routes of communication are not set in stone. Later, I became deputy clinical and then clinical director of medicine for the area subtended by the health authority. This was an important post as it allowed me to voice concerns of the physicians straight to the chief executive of the hospital as well as interacting with my physician colleagues to relay and discuss administrative proposals from management. I also attended the meeting of head of nursing staff chaired by a senior manager and several nurses responsible for different areas of nursing. The medical directorate had around 800 nurses so there were always problems to discuss. One area which was very important was the expenditure incurred by appointing agency nurses, usually because of sick leave and locum doctors (for the same reason). The cost to the health authority was very high and was constantly under discussion and review. Despite government promises to increase throughput of patients in a timely manner this cannot be achieved without an increase in staff even with the emergence of modern technology. I fully accept that authorities have written many books concerning reform of the NHS and that my perspective is limited to some extent. Nevertheless, I did gain sufficient clinical experience as well as an insight into management and budgeting to feel that I could comment.

A lot has happened since I retired from NHS practice in 2007 and it is sad to see the change in attitude of the GPs. They perceive the post as a job and not a vocation partly because they are under extreme pressure again due to lack of numbers. Morale is also variable in hospital staff for similar reasons and due to an ever-increasing workload eg. in accident and emergency units. The outbreak of Covid has not helped in these matters, indeed it has made pressures of staffing at all levels even worse. Also, there are so many different facets of the NHS from acute care to social care (critical) and public health to name but a few. Most GPs provide an excellent service, once you can see them. Patients being operated on in hospital for the most part have successful surgical procedures and are incredibly grateful. The British training system is particularly good although there are always improvements to be made. However, because it takes at least 10 years to train a medical student and sometimes more to consultant level one can appreciate the difficulties in promising great improvements tomorrow. The increase in bureaucracy and litigation does not help either. Several governments have increased NHS funding and this is to be welcomed. New hospitals have been built but resources are sadly lacking in some specialities eg. psychiatric services and cognate areas.

So what is the answer? There is no simple answer, but some comments may help. Firstly, the politics of NHS should be removed as far as possible. Secondly a national committee comprising representation from appropriate non-political bodies should be charged with determining the best way forward. This might include a form of private insurance, obviously an anathema to many NHS workers but a workable proposition in continental Europe. After all the majority of people in this country are employed so their employers could pay a bit towards this in addition to the health service charges they pay already. Of course, this would have economic consequences but should be discussed. It may free up resources if 'routine' surgical procedures such as hernia, cataract etc. were performed in a semiprivate setting thus removing stress on main hospital facilities. Several developments over the past decade or so are to be commended e.g., management of long-term illness by specialist nurses freeing up GPs, increasing delivery of surgery employing day care facilities and many others. Unfortunately, the fact remains that patient discharge and social care has required much more resource than has been available. The delivery of social care proceeds at a much slower pace than our ability to discharge patients from an acute hospital, resulting in significant delays and so called bed blocking. Combining the allocated budgets of these services may allow more control over the outcome.

Moving away from management issues I was privileged to be associated with many societies in UK, Europe and USA. In Cardiff, the Welsh Endocrine and Diabetic Society (WEDS) meets twice a year. The meeting lasts 1 day and papers and posters are presented together with a guest speaker usually from UK. It is a good way of networking endocrinologists working in Wales and is a relaxed and an enjoyable meeting. The Society of Physicians in Wales initially was restricted to general physicians and met twice a year, once in N Wales (at Portmeirion) and once in Cardiff. Again, it was a network group in addition to paper presentation. More recently it has expanded to include all physicians and specialists and serves as a source of information and opinion to the Welsh government. The Medical Research Society was a rigorous national organisation at which you were not allowed to look at notes of your presentation.

The Thyroid Club is a specialist society started after WW2. Early meetings consisted of a dinner in London followed by a talk and discussion which sometimes went on beyond closing time on the pavement. Initially it was restricted to consultants working in London only but this rule was relaxed when it became apparent that good thyroid clinical and experimental work was being performed in the provinces (e.g., in Glasgow and other centres). Over the years membership has grown and it was renamed The British Thyroid Association (BTA) but still retains independence from the Society of Endocrinology. I was fortunate and privileged to be elected as President of The BTA (2003-2005) and also to receive the George Murray prize medal for 2013 at which a lecture was presented in honour of the first physician to administer a thyroid preparation for treatment of hypothyroidism. Earlier in my career I was a staunch supporter of the British Thyroid Foundation which provides information on thyroid disease to the general public and is involved in various educational and fund-raising activities. In 2014 I was elected as a patron joining 8 others mostly non-medical personalities. I am still very proud to hold that position.

The European Thyroid Association (ETA) was founded in 1967 and has grown in membership from 200 or so to over 1000. It includes all who are interested in the thyroid gland including clinicians, basic scientists and other cognate specialties. There is an annual meeting in a different European country and the attendance has been increasing each year. I attended these meetings for nearly 50 years usually presenting papers. In 1993 the meeting was held in Cardiff and I assumed the chair of the organisation committee. In those days the meeting was for 5 days and included various dinners, excursions and a programme for nonparticipants (usually wives of members). It was a big task which was very successful. Subsequently I was elected as secretary treasurer of the association, a post with a 4 or 5 year duration. Membership of the ETA afforded the opportunity to forge both academic and social links over the years.

The Society of Endocrinology is now an amalgam of all specialist endocrine societies in UK. The annual meeting is large and speakers are invited from Europe and USA in addition to UK to give named lectures.

When I came to Cardiff in 1972 the only college of Physicians that was influential was the Royal College of Physicians of London. The college was very London oriented but over the decades it became clear that educational activities should take place in many provincial areas of the UK.

In Cardiff this involved the setting up of an RCP office and the presentation of a medical conference on general medicine for medical staff in Wales. This has proved very popular with a high attendance. In 2015, I was asked to deliver the Bradshaw Lecture, a named lecture of the RCP, which was a great honour. Tribute must be paid to my colleague Dr Howell Lloyd and others for their role in persuading the college to support educational medical events underpinned by the RCP outside London.

The Learned Society of Wales is a recently founded society which aims to be broadly equivalent to the Royal

Society of Edinburgh and The Royal Society in London. At present it has approximately 500 fellows from all academic disciplines, and I was elected in 2018.

CHAPTER 19

Teaching

Teaching the medical students and postgraduates was enjoyable, hard work and usually fun.

It was in the days before routine use of computers, so lectures were still an effective method of conveying information in a short time. The (? diligent) students took notes. The rest just sat and absorbed the content or caused mild havoc by heckling. Of course, with the advent of computer assisted learning the days of 100 to 150 students sitting in a lecture theatre have mostly disappeared.

The process and methodology of medical education was largely ignored by the powerful consultant body until the past 2-3 decades. The interest was sparked by the fact that the government woke up to the fact that medical education was quite varied between medical schools and expensive and that the government was funding it. I participated in medical education while in Glasgow at the behest of my colleague Ronald Harden who introduced me to The Association of The Study of Medical Education (ASME) which became a prime mover in the field. Ronald was a driving force in ASME. I continued my interest in Cardiff and served as Treasurer of ASME in the 1970s.

On moving to Cardiff, I served on various education committees in the medical and dental school and gained some appreciation of problems as seen by other heads of department, particularly in relation to any proposed curriculum change. I then became involved in helping to organise the final medical exams in Cardiff. Later on, I failed to be appointed as the dean of the medical school much to everyone's surprise. I was quite upset by this but took a new development route and became the secretary-treasurer of the European Thyroid Association which I probably would not have done had I been Dean. I also became involved as an examiner for the membership of the Royal College of Physicians in Glasgow and Edinburgh. This was hard work and consisted of examining students in 'short cases' and a long case as well as viva voce examination. I was once examining in Aberdeen and accompanying the host examiner when he decided to examine a candidate on patients sitting outside the ward on an informal basis. After this he asked me whether I would like to be a Fellow of the Royal College of Physicians of Edinburgh. On receiving my enthusiastic assent, he arranged this within weeks! Subsequently I became the Welsh representative to the Edinburgh college.

Back at home my first love was teaching medical students round the bedside of a patient. This is most rewarding whether it is first year of clinical exposure or in final year. It is the nearest thing to an apprenticeship system and the process gives you an accurate idea of the student's capabilities and knowledge. I believe these sessions have been curtailed because of "modern" teaching methods and this is a backward step in my view.

Early on in the Gardiner Institute of Medicine Western Infirmary Glasgow a lot of time was taken to produce teaching slide presentations under the guidance of Ronald Harden. He was a genuine enthusiast in medical education and eventually was awarded an OBE for his contributions to this field in UK and abroad. Of course, with the advent of computerised learning and all the technology that has resulted from that, the delivery of medical education has changed completely.

CHAPTER 20

Retirement (1)

Retirement came after 40 years as a practising doctor. Hitherto it had to be taken at age 65 usually in the September before the academic year commenced. At that time (2007) this requirement was being relaxed and I wondered whether I should make a fuss and continue. After some thought I decided that enough was enough and so 2 months before my 66th birthday I retired. A new life had begun. The University Superannuation Scheme pension arrangements were much more generous than those of today. At the time of retiral the department in University Hospital arranged an informal party which was delightful. The following year my colleagues Dr. (now Prof) Peter Smyth from Dublin and Dr (now Prof) Marian Ludgate arranged a festschrift for me which was a splendid event. Firstly, there was an afternoon of lectures given by authorities in the thyroid field from Cardiff, Sheffield, and Cambridge, I was also very honoured to have friends and colleagues from New York, Boston and The Mayo Clinic arrive to give talks all relating to some of my activities and interests in the thyroid field. Eventually all this was published in an Endocrine journal. After the talks we repaired to a top-class hotel in Cardiff overlooking Cardiff Bay for dinner and some entertaining speeches. I am pleased to thank Dr Bernard Rees Smith for his financial support for this meeting. A splendid and memorable day not to be forgotten. The next day we hosted a luncheon party at our home for friends and visitors from abroad.

I had decided to do private work and started at an office just along the road where we lived. I enjoyed this as I was able to devote more time to the patient and I think many were very grateful for this. The diseases were mainly thyroid related. However, eventually the referrals began to reduce in number, and I thought it better to stop. However, I was still supervising the large trial of thyroxine in pregnant women (The CATS Study) and this continued till the paper was published in 2012.

I was also busy being involved in around 60 publications (papers, book chapters, guidelines etc) from 2007 – 2012. At that point I decided to relinquish my licence to practise with the General Medical Council and was therefore casting around for other activities. At that time, I had helped to organise a meeting on iodine deficiency in Europe held in London under the auspices of the International Council for Control of Iodine Deficiency Disorders (ICCIDD).

Back in Cardiff my friend Dr Howell Lloyd put me forward to join the committee of Tenovus (now Tenovus Cancer Care). This organisation, formed to help cancer victims has been operative since World War 2 and founded by ten men (hence the name) who had clubbed together during World War2 in Cardiff to buy essential items for a friend who was in hospital suffering from cancer. After he passed away the group continued to raise funds to provide essential items for poor people who were ill and could not provide for themselves or their families. Operating mainly in Wales it provides assistance to patients of modest means to help them obtain appropriate therapy and living aids. It was exciting for me being part of the so-called 3rd sector involved in fund raising as well as spending resource on such items as mobile chemotherapy units and supervision of charity shops the length and breadth of Wales in addition to some in England which sold second hand goods.

This was the first time I had been involved in the charity sector so I was on a steep learning curve. I was concerned to learn that up to one hundred charities per week were being dissolved in the UK. The role of the charity commission in overseeing the governance of charities in UK is critical and every so often a scandal is reported relating to inadequate governance and or faulty financial management; nevertheless, most charities are well meaning and devoted to their cause. This is certainly the case with Tenovus Cancer Care and I learnt a lot being on the management board with a diverse group of people. Later on, I became vice-chairman and worked closely with the chairman, Richard Sims a businessman, and Claudia McVie, the executive director. A development which occurred when I was there was the introduction of choirs involving local communities which was recognised nationally. The launch of more mobile units for chemotherapy administration was also welcomed by patients who had difficulty attending the hospital in their area. I met a new set of dedicated staff as well as the trustees who were from diverse backgrounds and brought different skills to the table.

The annual income of the charity (in 2017) was about 8 million pounds; in order to generate this income required a lot of hard work by many people. In addition to the standard methods of bucket collections in the street at events such as rugby matches, football matches and other sporting fixtures two important strategies were employed. One involves the acquisition and management of around 60 charity shops distributed over Wales and also in adjoining parts of England. This is a huge retail organisation which receives goods from the public to sell in the shops and sells any remnants on the rag market. The shops are profitable for the most part but there are always issues relating to staff retention and rent. A more recent development has been the formation of choirs comprised of cancer patients and their relatives (mentioned above). This caught the excitement of many populations across Wales resulting in enthusiastic participation and appearances on TV and national competitions. The publicity was invaluable. While the income did not match that of the retail outlets it does provide a community focus and even contributes to some research projects performed within the organisation.

Is all this activity worthwhile? I would endorse this very strongly. The income supports several basic science projects addressing cancer genetics as well as some clinical aspects of cancer therapy. It also provides support for those with cancer and limited means to improve their quality of life (providing a washing machine or a heater etc). A relatively recent development has been the introduction of mobile chemotherapy units in conjunction with the local cancer service and/or hospital; these units which are the size of a single decker bus can access remote parts of Wales and deliver cancer chemotherapy on site. This is obviously a great boon to cancer sufferers who have difficulty travelling to a cancer centre.

The board of management functioned well but occasionally had some difficult issues to face nearly all of which related to personnel. No long-term damage was perceived but I learnt that appropriate advice from legal and other qualified sources was essential. In this type of organisation there is a time limit on board membership and, while I was sad to depart, I hoped that my contribution was helpful.

CHAPTER 21

Retirement (2)

Iodine Deficiency

Early in my association with Tenovus Cancer Care I co-hosted a meeting on iodine deficiency in London mostly pertaining to UK. The favoured method of delivering iodine to an iodine deficient population is by adding it to salt used in commercial and domestic consumption. It is nothing short of a scandal that this has not been done in UK as it is known, for example, that sub normal maternal iodine concentration in pregnancy can adversely affect foetal and infant development particularly with regard to brain development. There is a world organisation devoted to advocating normal iodine status in all countries known as International Council for Control of Iodine Deficiency Disorders (ICCIDD) with a regional coordinator for each group of countries (e.g., Europe, Asia etc). Unfortunately, Prof Aldo Pinchera, based in Pisa, the regional coordinator of ICCIDD in Europe could not attend and sadly he passed away in October 2012. He was a larger-than-life role model for many of us with an encyclopaedic knowledge of the thyroid and endocrinology, a great extrovert, a consummate endocrinologist with a large department and a skilled politician.

A week or so after his death I was asked to succeed him as European coordinator of ICCIDD soon to be renamed

The Iodine Global Network (IGN). I made some enquiries and then indicated that I was honoured and delighted to accept the role. The IGN operated from Ottawa, Canada and had approximately 10 to 14 regional coordinators worldwide acting as a management council (MC) together with many national coordinators as well as a board of trustees. The MC meets once per year in various locations the last one being in Lima, Peru in 2020 just before the pandemic of Covid struck. Being responsible for Europe involved assessment of iodine status in five hundred million people and making recommendations for harmonisation. This has proved a challenging task as there are few laws that can be followed by any one country. There are also varying levels of iodine between countries. Since iodine deficiency during pregnancy is associated with neurocognitive impairment in childhood it became apparent that advocacy to health authorities, public health bodies and governments to achieve appropriate iodine status was critical. Despite these problems huge progress has been made in providing adequate iodine status in many countries round the world during the past 25-30 years and this will have long term beneficial effects on the intellectual development of children and the economy in general.

Again, I began a steep learning curve into nutrition, public health and the European Union (UK was still a member then). At that time there were 10 regional coordinators in the world, and we met once a year in different world locations such as Bangkok, Delhi, London and Dakar as the management council. This was a great opportunity for networking and reporting on progress (or lack of it in my case) on the iodine situation in one's region. In 2015 I organised the IGN meeting in London held at a hotel near Lords cricket ground. I took the opportunity to arrange an excursion to Greenwich which was highly successful. An additional feature was that some members of the board of IGN attended which gave the members of the management council the chance to meet and discuss. Most of the regional coordinators were not medical doctors and all had different backgrounds, so we learnt from each other. The meetings only lasted 3 days and then the delegates either travelled home or took advantage of the location to take some vacation. After around 8 years of stimulating and enjoyable work for IGN I decided to tender my resignation, as it happened, just before the Covid crisis. I believe now that most of the meetings are conducted by Zoom.

During my so-called retirement I was in constant demand to review scientific papers; far too many requests arrived so I had to be selective. This was demanding work which received no recognition and when I retired again, I ceased all activity in this regard. Also, I had been involved in many projects and since 2007 my name has appeared on more than one hundred publications.

CHAPTER 22

The End Game

As the sign says on the boards carried up and down Sauchiehall street in Glasgow "The End is Nigh"! Fortunately, we are not there yet. In autumn 2020 Maureen and I both contracted Covid. I only just avoided hospital admission and do not seem to have any symptoms of long Covid. Maureen recovered fully in a few days. However, while in the recovery phase I was diagnosed as having cancer of the Prostate and have subsequently been treated with radiotherapy and androgen deprivation therapy. To date (nearly 36 months following completion of radiotherapy) there is no evidence of progression. During this period, we have celebrated our 50th wedding anniversary and my 80th birthday.

What of my career? People say that I should have been appointed Dean of the Medical School and that I should have also been up graded to Professor sooner than I was. However, I am fairly resilient and I turned my activities to Europe (as suggested at the time by Reg Hall) and am proud to have been known throughout the continent as an authority on thyroid disease in pregnancy. My grandfather Lazarus said to me when I was about 14 "Just do an honest day's work" and I have tried to abide by that. My colleagues and I often say we had the best of times in Medicine which I believe to be true.

I enjoyed nearly all of it although the administration was a bit tedious at times.

CHAPTER 23

The Family

My family tree is quite complex. None of my grandparents was born in UK and all were from large or very large families.

I will document my close family first, then the origins of the wider groups followed by an account of Maureen's family.

Lazarus Family

My paternal grandfather was Isaac Lazarus who was the eldest of seven children. He was one of two siblings to be born in Lithuania in 1881. The country was under the direct rule of the Russian Empire. At that time there were frequent antisemitic pogroms. Troops of Cossacks or other horsebound military would swoop into a small village, shoot a few people and then set fire to the whole village. The pogroms and the official reaction to them led many Russian Jews to reassess their perceptions of their status within the Russian Empire, and so led to significant Jewish emigration, mostly to the United States. Grandpa's village was razed to the ground and his father (Hersh Leizer Melamud) decided that the family should emigrate. It is highly likely that Hirsch-Leizer and his wife were deeply affected by the pogroms in their part of what is now Lithuania and decided to move to UK. But what was it about them apart from having contacts in Glasgow that drove them to emigrate? After all many from the same population and circumstances chose not to follow this path. I am sure that the reasons are many but the growth of their family was assured by residence in UK whereas those populations who stayed in their country of birth in Eastern Europe were obliterated during WW2.

However, in the latter part of the 19th century more than two million people fled to The United States, mainly New York City. My great grandfather had several siblings, most of whom did indeed travel to USA/Canada. Meanwhile my great grandfather arrived in Leith docks on the East coast of Scotland in the late 1880s and was asked his name at the port. Hirsch Leizer M'lamoud he replied. The port official immediately said 'your name is Harris Lazarus'. He was able then to travel to Glasgow and proceeded to continue with his family and enter into business. There are relatives in The United States called Teacher (the translation of Melamud) and one (Brian Teacher from California) reached the quarter final of Wimbledon tennis championship in the 1980s. As seen from the figure Isaac had six siblings. My father Samuel Lazarus was born on 22nd July 1911, the third child of Isaac and Rebecca (nee Gerber). The eldest child, Joe died aged twelve of Rheumatic fever and the second child, Hilda died aged sixteen from encephalitis 6 weeks after being admitted to hospital in Newcastle. Of course, many families in The UK suffered similar tragedies early in the 20th century but my grandma never really got over this one and I don't think I ever saw her not in a black dress for the rest of her life. The youngest child was Eve (see family tree). The family lived in Queens Park on the South side of Glasgow. Isaac was a jeweller but had met my grandmother Rebecca (Becky) Gerber while both were working at WO and DH Wills tobacco manufacturing plant on the north side of Glasgow.

They married on January 8th 1901. Isaac was a committed Zionist and attended the 8th Zionist congress in Amsterdam in 1908. The family moved to Newcastle -on-Tyne after World War I to set up a business with Gerber Brothers who were trading in Glasgow.

Isaac had three brothers and three sisters. One brother died from Tuberculosis in 1913. The next oldest lost his first wife at the birth of their son in Glasgow. He remarried, had two children and emigrated to New York in the 1920s with his wife and three children. The family settled there and his eldest, Joe, became a businessman; his daughter, Muriel became a scientist and later a psychoanalyst. Her younger brother, Sydney studied medicine and became a pathologist. Isaac's youngest brother emigrated to Canada but developed severe psychiatric disease and was sent back to Glasgow where he remained in a long-term psychiatric facility until he died in his 60s. He was unmarried. The three sisters all married and had successful families.

My father attended The Royal Grammar School in Newcastle and was clearly bright and industrious. The commercial venture with Gerber brothers did not work out and in 1928 the family moved back to Glasgow and my father started medical studies at The University. He was just 17 and 2 months. He lived at home on the South side of Glasgow during his undergraduate career and travelled by tram to classes every day. Occasionally he was late for the Botany lecture which started at 8am with no entry to the lecture theatre after that time so he played billiards till 9am! He was a hardworking and assiduous student who graduated in 1933 with commendation. Following 2 resident (house officer) posts he enrolled to study for a higher degree. He joined the physiology department in Glasgow which was chaired by Professor EP Cathcart. Cathcart had been instrumental in helping to ensure that the wartime population on UK achieved adequate (though minimal) nutrition. Sam studied the transport of various substances through the intestine of animals and was awarded MD with high commendation in 1936. During this time, he was able to do several locum jobs in general practice as well as study for his membership examination of the royal college of Physicians examination to be taken in London. He passed the MRCP at the first attempt (a signal achievement) and embarked on a tour of different medical departments. First, he went to Copenhagen, Denmark in October 1936 to study under the famed Professor Meulengracht. He then attended Guys Hospital in London April 1937 to gain gastroenterological experience with Sir Arthur Hurst before returning to Glasgow. He was appointed Professor of Pharmacology and Therapeutics at Anderson College (one of Glasgow's 3 medical schools) just before World War Two and remained in Glasgow during the war. While in London he had met Thelma Viner at a dinner party and they married on 8th January 1941 when he was 29. It was not until that day that he discovered that his parents also had been married on the same day 40 years earlier.

After the war, the inception of the National Health Service in 1948 was accompanied by the cessation of the two additional medical colleges in Glasgow. Sam was appointed as honorary lecturer in Materia Medica but worked as an NHS physician. He had a flourishing private practice in the Jewish community in the city and was an examiner for the Glasgow and Edinburgh colleges of Physicians in the membership examination. He was always fair and charming, attitudes which gave him the epithet of the smiling ploughman! Following retirement in 1976 he continued with some private practice and involved himself in charity work and travel.

My mother, Thelma Viner was born on 3rd April 1918 in Sheffield. She had no siblings. In contrast to my father's family her parents were wealthy, her father Emile having co-founded Viners, the cutlery and silverware manufacturer in Sheffield. Emile was the second youngest of 13 children and had 4 brothers and 8 sisters, but one died in infancy. Rose Herbert married Emile in 1917. She had one sister, Beatrice and 5 brothers. Thelma went to boarding school on the south coast at Eastbourne when she was 11 years old and loved it. In her teenage years her parents had a flat in central London as well as a house in Sheffield. Following matriculation exams, she attended College Montmorency in Paris and attained a diploma in French Language and Literature as well as History of art and dramatic art.

Back in London she then attended The Chelsea Polytechnic (now not in existence) to study Botany but never graduated as she met my father and also World War 2 started. Her parents had now bought a large (mainly Georgian) villa (Stoke Hall) south of Sheffield and she got married from there aged 22 on January 8th 1941.

Lazarus Family Tree

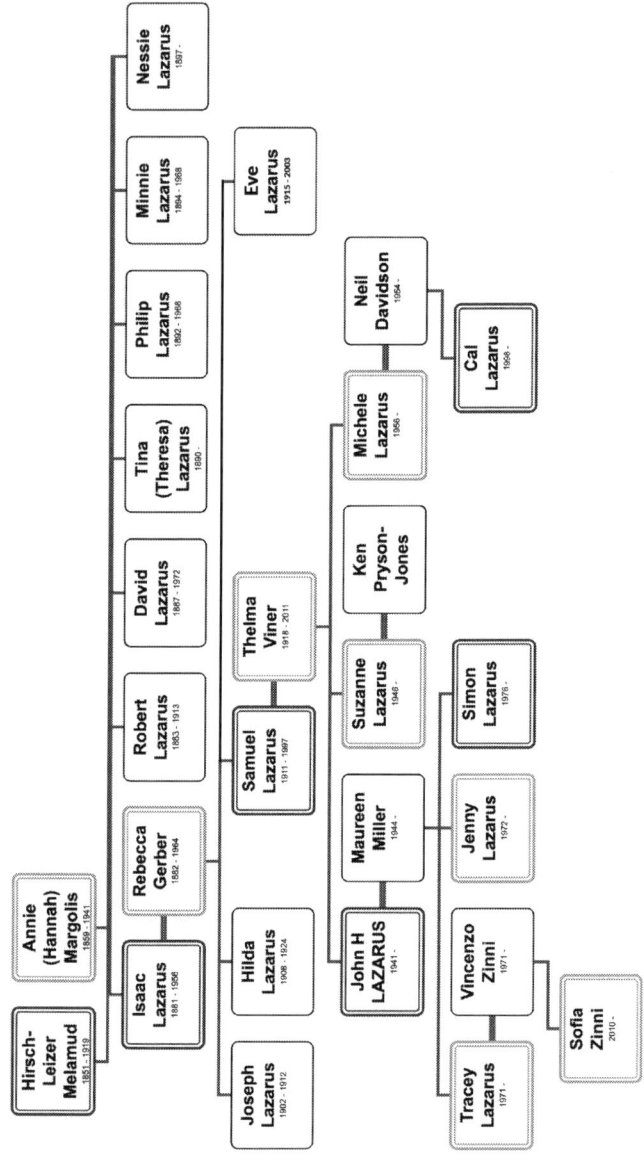

114

Gerber Family

My Close Family

Maureen and I have 3 children, Tracey who is an arts consultant, Jenny who is a General Practitioner and Simon who is in aerospace engineering. Tracey and Vincenzo have 1 daughter, Sofia. Vincenzo is currently the chairman of an Aluminium company in Italy. They all live in England not more than 1 and a half hours away from our house in Cardiff which is very convenient. Maureen's father, James Miller, was a county architect (Dunbartonshire) and her mother an art teacher who trained at Glasgow School of Art. Maureen had an older sister, Pat, who also trained at Glasgow School of Art and won prizes for her embroidery. She met her husband Ian at The School of Art and had 3 children. Pat died at the early age of 32. Maureen trained as a teacher in Glasgow but when we moved to Cardiff she worked in adult literacy. She then studied for a degree at the Open University and in due course achieved a BA (Hons) in Arts.

Maureen and I at Compton Verney

This eventually took her to The National Museum and Galleries in Cardiff where she found employment as an assistant conservator. Following the discovery of many interesting old botanical prints in the botany storeroom of the Botany Dept., she and her colleagues realised the high significance of these in the world of Botanical Art. This led to an exhibition in 1996-7 entitled 'The Paradise Garden' which was highly successful. A book, of the same title, was published to accompany the exhibition. Later, they produced the 'Catalogue of Botanical Prints and Drawings at the National Museum and Galleries of Wales in 2003'. Subsequently she has written papers about aspects of botanical art in the collection in the 17th and 18th centuries and has also been asked to lecture in various locations. She became an FLS (Fellow of the Linnaean Society), a signal honour, in 2007.

The Gerbers

My father's mother was Rebecca (Grandma Beck) Gerber, the fifth child of Joseph and Sarah Gerber. She had three older sisters, one older brother and 2 younger brothers. They came from Riga, Latvia where Joseph was in the umbrella trade. He died when he was forty from disease of the gallbladder.

The remaining family then thought of emigrating to USA and to make a start. Enough money was saved to purchase a ticket for the eldest child, Pauline, to travel to New York. The aim was for Pauline to earn enough money to purchase tickets for all of them to follow her. Pauline was an industrious seamstress and in due course sent tickets for the rest of the family. The umbrella shop was sold, and Mrs Gerber arrived at the docks in Riga with her remaining 6 children. At this point she had serious doubts about travelling and living in New York. She decided it was not religious enough for her and the children. She then went back to Riga city and luckily the person who had bought the shop was persuaded to sell it back to her. Pauline was aghast at the news but did stay connected with her family. She had married and had three sons. Eventually Sarah Gerber received an invitation from a certain Moses Woolfson to come to Glasgow and live with him. Later on, Moses's son Philip married Sarah's daughter Clara Gerber. Sarah duly arrived in Glasgow and the Woolfson and Gerber families became very close.

Riga was a large city on the Baltic with a substantial population. It is interesting that family were residing there as the law was that it was restricted to non-Jews in the main. Riga was an art nouveau city and very elegant. Unfortunately, when the Nazis arrived in World War II, they used Riga as a collection point for Jews rounded up in other parts of the country and also from outside the country. In Riga they started to kill them. They even crammed a synagogue with hundreds of Jews, locked the doors and set fire to the building. My grandma Beck lost many family members who never left Riga before the war despite entreaties from my grandfather to leave before the war and go to United Kingdom or United States of America. Initially I did not wish to go to Riga but later in my career I did go and even organised a thyroid meeting there in 2008.

My mother Thelma (right) accompanying my grandfather (Isaac) and grandmother (Becky) to a function in Glasgow in the early 1940's or 50's.

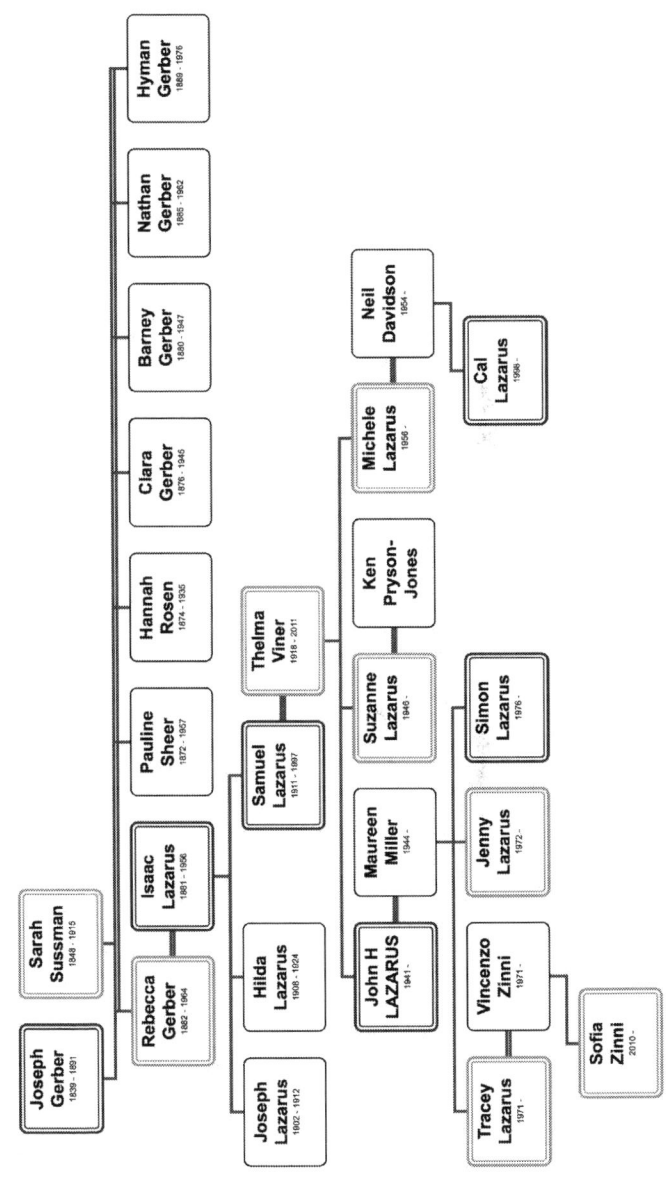

The Wieners (Viners)

My great grandmother (Amalia Furst) was born in Bremerhaven, Germany and died in Norwich England in 1898 after having thirteen children. One died in infancy. All the children were born in Germany including my grandfather Emil who was born in Bremerhaven in 1888. For some reason Amalia thought the obstetric doctors there were better than in Norwich and she stayed there for 6 weeks after the birth. Emil was brought up by his two eldest sisters in London as his mother died in 1898.

The Wiener family in the early 20th century.
Two members of the family are missing from this photograph.

Their sisters and Emil left school at fourteen years and continued to live with some siblings in London before Emil went on the road to sell merchandise. He then moved to Sheffield as some relatives were already there. In the early 1900s the cutlery and holloware industry was very fragmented. The meant that one shop (or even household) would be stamping out forks and another would be buffing them and yet another would be polishing and so on. Emil and a brother (Adolph) saw an opportunity to bring all these skills under one roof resulting in more efficient production and economy. This approach proved to be successful and Viners began to grow. In 1923 his name was changed to Viner (instead of Wiener) and his forename to Emile (from Emil). In the 1930s Emile was given a Royal Warrant as a supplier of cutlery to King George V and the Royal household. During the second world war the company made tin helmets, bullets, bayonets and packed parachutes as well as sustaining bomb and incendiary damage. Post war Emile presided over a highly successful company selling in many parts of the world and employing up to 1000 people. It was a public company and was listed on the London stock exchange. However, during the mid to late 70s the British market was inundated with Korean and Japanese imports of stainless-steel items. The public taste for silver declined and eventually the company was sold and resold. Today the name lives on but attached to quite different products from 70 years ago.

By this time Emile had reached the age of 70 and retired as chairman and sold his shares in the company. He had lived in Sheffield for more than 50 years and had developed chronic obstructive lung disease (chronic bronchitis) partly due to the pollution in Sheffield during the time and partly due to cigarette smoking. Accordingly, he moved to Bournemouth with Rose and died after her in 1978 aged 90.

Wiener/Viner Family Tree

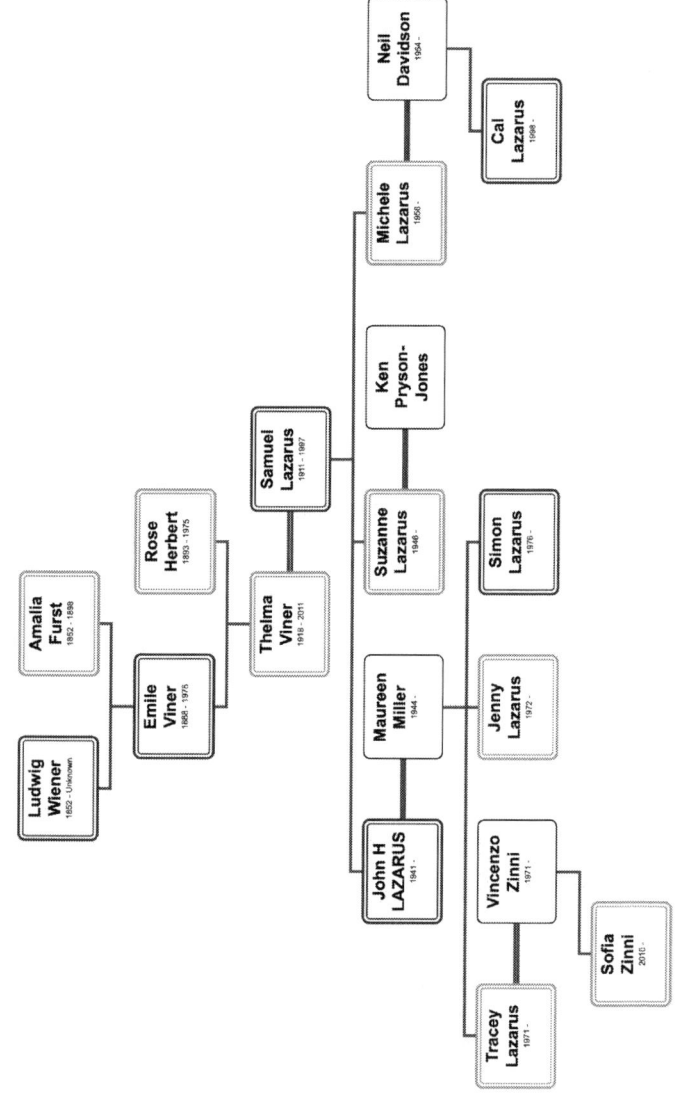

The Herberts/Strausslers

My mother's mother was Rose Herbert, but she was born Rose Straussler (see family tree) in Cape Town, S. Africa. Her mother, Jane Goldberg was born in London and married Leopold Straussler, a Hungarian, in 1884. Where and how they met is not clear, but the marriage was in London. Leopold's occupation was given as a furrier like his father.

Leopold had a brother who was a doctor, possibly a neurologist, living in Budapest with his mother. Leopold and his wife eventually settled in Hungary, and it is thought he managed large tracts of forest on the Hungarian Romanian border. It is probable the family travelled to S Africa several times where Leopold had business affairs and several of the children were born there. Tragedy then struck when Leopold was allegedly murdered in Hungary although there is no proof of this in Hungarian records. At the same time, the factor of the estate, who was antisemitic, stole a large amount of money and fled to San Francisco. My great grandma Jean (as she was known) sent her eldest son Fred to San Francisco to search for him but both he and the factor were never heard of again. It is thought that Fred may have perished in the 1906 earthquake which killed around three thousand people. Following this momentous event my great grandmother. now a widow with 6 children. returned to London and changed her surname to Herbert. She had enough money to send the children to private school and she eventually opened a fashion shop in Regent Street.

Her youngest child Leonard was in the family business but also a champagne socialist. He and his elder brother, John, were in the infantry during World War 1 and fought in the trenches. His mother sent Leonard to Cardiff in 1928 to open a dress shop on the main street. No one foresaw the arrival of his great nephew (myself) in the same city approximately 45 years later. The dress shop was said to be one of the two best in the city. However, Leonard gave this up in 1936 to go and fight in the Spanish civil war on the communist side and survived this experience to return to London before the outbreak of World War Two. He lived with his older brother John in London and both retired to Hove in Sussex. An elder brother died in a car accident near Leicester in 1923.

Leopold Straussler (my great grandfather) had a brother Adolphus in Budapest. He had a son Nicholas (b 1891) who moved to London to study engineering in the early 1900s. He then became interested in development of tanks that could float as well as travel on ground and his designs were used on D Day with favourable effect. He died in 1966 and his obituary was in The Times.

Herberts/Strausslers Family Tree

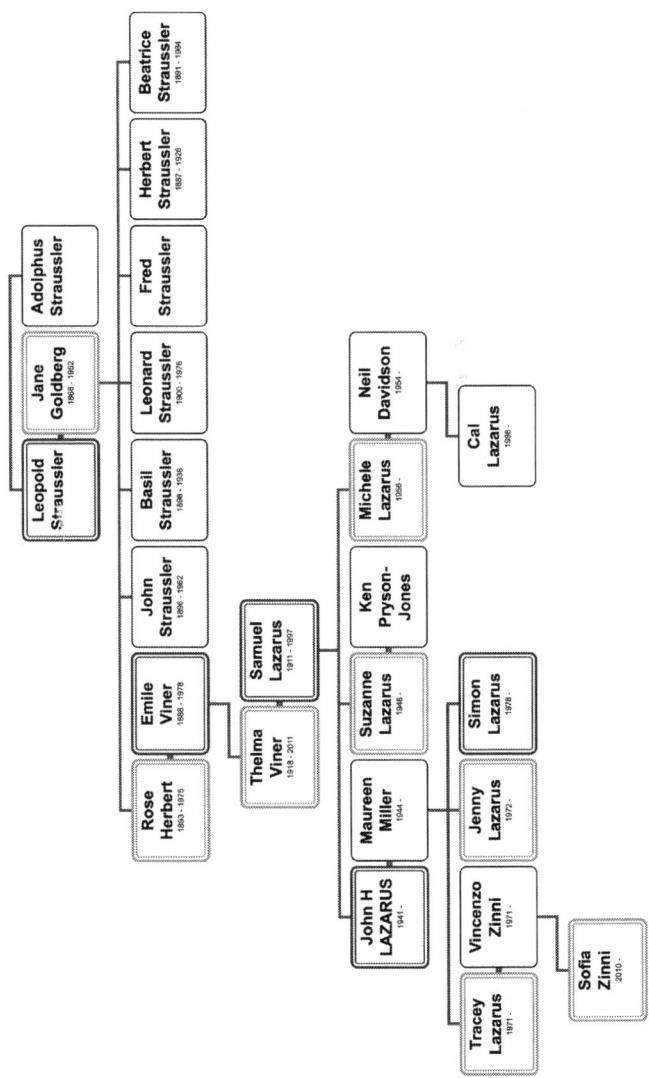

Maureen's family (Miller)

Maureen's father (James) was the middle son of three and became an architect after studying at night in the Glasgow School of Art. He served in the army during World War 2 and was posted to India. At art school he met his future wife Molly McKenzie and married before the war. Their first child Patricia (Pat) was born while they were living in Dundee. After the war the family moved to live in the South side of Glasgow eventually moving to Helensburgh on the river Clyde. Meanwhile, Maureen had been born in 1944 and went to school in the South side of the city. Maureen's mother had attended Glasgow Art School during the 1930s as had her younger sister Normana. They both became schoolteachers. Pat also attended Glasgow School of Art where she had a distinguished career winning prizes in Embroidery. She met Ian Ross at the art school and they married in 1963. He was a commercial designer working latterly for The Marquess of Bute who ran a cloth mill. The eldest of the McKenzie sisters (Alla) did not have an artistic talent but did attend Glasgow University and read French and Spanish. She became a schoolteacher and had one son after her marriage to Matt McKibben, himself a schoolteacher. Maureen attended Jordan Hill college of education to train as a schoolteacher and then taught in an inner city primary school and subsequently at a school near Helensburgh.

Meanwhile James had become the county architect for Dunbartonshire. Pat had 3 children, twin boys and a girl before she very sadly died aged thirty-two

in 1971. Ian married again to Thelma Robertson and had a girl, Caroline who has two children.

Later on the eldest twin, Giles, died in his early twenties, another tragedy.

Miller Family Tree

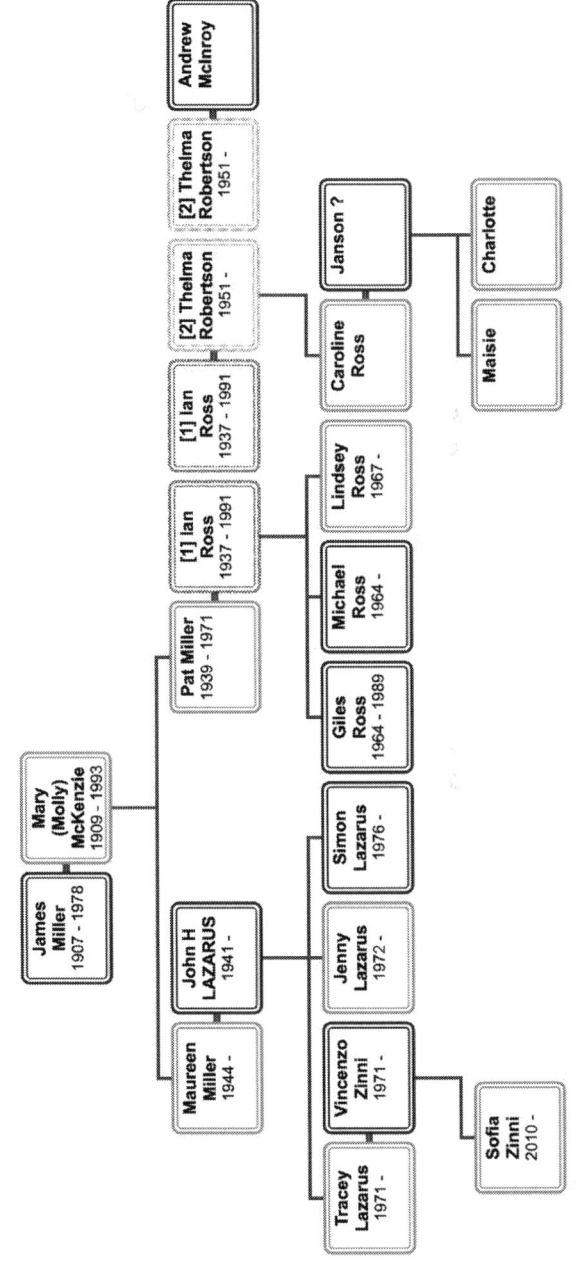

127

Acknowledgements

This book would not have come to fruition without the help of many people to whom I am incredibly grateful. Of course, any errors are purely my responsibility.

My wife Maureen, while providing loving support throughout the years, helped with proof reading and our three children (Tracey, Jenny and Simon) assisted with information and computing.

I also owe a huge debt to Janis Hickey, former founder and director British Thyroid Foundation for the family trees. I would like to thank my sisters Suzanne Prysor Jones and Michele Lazarus for information. Hazel Woolfson, my first cousin, has done extensive research into the family trees and I am very grateful to her for some details. Thanks go to my medical secretaries including Sue Baker, Heather Thomas, Gaynor Williams and many others I would also like to record my grateful thanks to medical colleagues who supported me during my journey. The late Prof Sir Edward Wayne and the late Prof Graham Wilson from The Department of Medicine at The Western Infirmary Glasgow. Also at this location include the late Dr Donald Alexander and Prof Ronald Harden as well as many junior colleagues. In the department of Medicine at Columbia University New York I am grateful to the late Prof Ken Sterling and Dr Peter Mich for help and advice. In Cardiff I thank Prof Malcolm Wheeler, endocrine surgeon for inviting me to be a co editor of a well reviewed volume on The Thyroid and the late Prof Reg Hall for providing enthusiasm and drive. I apologise if I have omitted anyone from this list.